Mozambique:

Malaria Operational Plan FY 2014

Table of Contents

ABBREVIATIONS

ACT	Artemisinin-based combination therapy
AIDS	Acquired immune deficiency syndrome
AL	Artemether-lumefantrine
ANC	Antenatal clinic
APE	*Agentes Polivalentes Elementares da Saúde* (Community-based healthcare worker)
BCC	Behavior change communications
CDC	Centers for Disease Control and Prevention
CMAM	*Central de Medicamentos e Artigos Médicos* (Central Medical Stores)
DEPROS	*Departamento de Promoção de Saúde* (Health Promotion Department)
DHS	Demographic and Health Survey
DPS	*Direcção Provincial de Saúde* (Provincial Health Department)
EPI	Expanded Program on Immunization
FELTP	Field Epidemiology & Laboratory Training Program
FY	Fiscal year
Global Fund	Global Fund to Fight AIDS, Tuberculosis, and Malaria
GHI	Global Health Initiative
GoM	Government of Mozambique
IMVCS	Integrated Malaria Vector Control Strategy
HIV	Human immunodeficiency virus
IPTp	Intermittent preventive treatment of pregnant women
INS	*Instituto Nacional de Saúde* (National Institute of Health)
INSIDA	*Inquérito de Indicadores de SIDA* (AIDS Indicator Survey)
IRS	Indoor residual spraying
ITN	Insecticide-treated bed net
LLIN	Long-lasting insecticide-treated bed net
LMIS	Logistics Management Information Systems
MACEPA	Malaria Control and Evaluation Partnerships in Africa
M&E	Monitoring and evaluation
MCH	Maternal and Child Health
MICS	Multiple Indicator Cluster Survey
MIP	Malaria in pregnancy
MIS	Malaria Indicator Survey
MISAU	*Ministério de Saúde* (Ministry of Health)
MOP	Malaria Operational Plan
NMCP	*Programa Nacional de Controlo da Malária* (National Malaria Control Program)
PEPFAR	President's Emergency Plan for AIDS Relief
PIRCOM	*Programa Inter-Religioso contra a Malária* (Inter-Religious Campaign Against Malaria)
PMI	President's Malaria Initiative
RDT	Rapid diagnostic test
SP	Sulfadoxine pyrimethamine
UNICEF	United Nations Children's Fund

USAID   United States Agency for International Development
USG   U.S. Government
WHO   World Health Organization

EXECUTIVE SUMMARY

Malaria prevention and control are major foreign assistance objectives of the U.S. Government. In May 2009, President Barack Obama announced the Global Health Initiative (GHI), a six-year, comprehensive effort to reduce the burden of disease and promote healthy communities and families around the world. Through GHI, the United States will help partner countries improve health outcomes, with a particular focus on improving the health of women, newborns, and children.

The President's Malaria Initiative (PMI) is a core component of the GHI, along with HIV/AIDS and tuberculosis. PMI was launched in June 2005 as a five-year, $1.2 billion initiative to rapidly scale up malaria prevention and treatment interventions and reduce malaria-related mortality by 50% in 15 high-burden countries in sub-Saharan Africa. With passage of the 2008 Lantos-Hyde Act, funding for PMI was extended and, as part of GHI, the goal of PMI was adjusted to reduce malaria-related mortality by 70% in the original 15 countries by the end of 2015. Programming of PMI activities follows the core principles of GHI.

Mozambique was selected as a PMI country in fiscal year (FY) 2007. PMI's primary goal in Mozambique is to assist the Government of Mozambique (GoM), in collaboration with other partners, to reduce malaria mortality by 50% by rapidly scaling-up coverage of vulnerable groups with four highly effective interventions: artemisinin-based combination therapy (ACT), intermittent preventive treatment of pregnant women (IPTp), insecticide-treated bed nets (ITNs), and indoor residual spraying (IRS).

Mozambique carried out a Demographic and Health Survey (DHS) in 2011. While the data from this survey did show a reduction in all cause under-five mortality from 138/1000 in the 2008 Multiple Indicator Cluster Survey to 97/1000 in the 2011 DHS, there were only minimal improvements in major malaria indicators compared to the 2007 Malaria Indicator Survey (MIS), highlighting the multitude of challenges the country still faces in reducing the burden of malaria. The most significant improvement from the 2007 MIS to the 2011 DHS was the increase in net coverage: the proportion of households with at least one ITN increased from 15.8% in 2007 to 51.4% in 2011. A joint Malaria Indicator Survey and National HIV/AIDS Indicator Survey is planned for 2014.

Mozambique has received several rounds of funding from the Global Fund to Fight AIDS, Tuberculosis, and Malaria (Global Fund). Mozambique was most recently awarded a $63 million Global Fund Round 9 grant to scale up universal access to malaria prevention and control services. The first phase of this grant began in July 2011 and ended in June 2013. This grant has two principal recipients: the Ministry of Health (MISAU) and World Vision Mozambique. The MISAU grant focused on procurement of commodities, including long-lasting insecticide treated nets (LLINs), insecticides for IRS, rapid diagnostic tests (RDTs), and ACTs. It also provided funding to World Vision to conduct activities at the community level in seven out of Mozambique's eleven provinces, including LLIN distribution, and implementation of behavior change communication (BCC) activities to promote prevention and treatment-seeking behaviors. Mozambique's proposal for the second phase of the Global Fund Round 9 grant was recently accepted and will run from July 2013 through June 2016, with a total funding of $85 million. The second phase will be directed towards procurement and distribution of nets to achieve universal coverage, procurement of insecticide for the national IRS program, procurement of RDTs and ACTs, BCC activities, monitoring and evaluation (M&E) support, and refresher training for community health workers. The PMI Mozambique team worked closely with the principal recipients during the development of the Round 9 Phase 2 application to ensure synergies with PMI-supported activities in the country.

This FY 2014 PMI Malaria Operational Plan (MOP) for Mozambique was developed during a planning visit in May 2013 by representatives from the U.S. Agency for International Development, the Centers for Disease Control and Prevention, and the National Malaria Control Program (NMCP), with participation from other major partners working on malaria in Mozambique. The proposed PMI activities with FY 2014 funding are based on progress and experiences during the last six years and the NMCP's 2012-2016 National Malaria Control Strategy. The majority of activities outlined in this FY 2014 MOP are based on strategic shifts in PMI activities that were begun in the FY 2013 MOP and approved FY 2013 reprogramming.

In order to achieve the greatest impact at the lowest levels of the health system, the PMI program in Mozambique has begun to decentralize many of its activities down to the provincial and district levels where possible, beginning with FY 2013 funds and continuing with this MOP. In addition, PMI will begin to support the national IRS program to help ensure a high quality of spraying nationwide while continuing the PMI-funded spray program in Zambézia. PMI will also expand its support of the routine LLIN distribution system by including distribution to children through the Expanded Program on Immunization and will look into complementary continuous distribution methods in the future. To ensure nets reach their intended recipients through the routine distribution system, PMI will set up a temporary, semi-parallel system while providing support to strengthen the government's system, allowing for an eventual transfer of responsibilities. PMI activities are designed to complement activities supported by other partners.

Over the past 18 months, the GoM has made significant progress, with support from PMI and other partners, in the finalization and dissemination of key strategic documents, including the 2012-2016 National Malaria Control Strategy, the National M&E Plan, the National Communication Strategic Plan for Malaria, the National Strategy for Improving and Sustaining LLIN Coverage, and the draft Integrated Malaria Vector Control Strategy.

The total amount of PMI funding requested for Mozambique is $29 million for FY 2014 and the following activities are planned:

Insecticide-treated nets: Since its launch in Mozambique in 2007, PMI has supported free LLIN distribution, primarily through antenatal clinics (ANC), with limited support to mass campaigns. As in previous years, in 2012, PMI procured enough insecticide-treated nets to cover needs for routine ANC distribution (~1.3 million nets) and will do so again in 2013. With FY 2014 funding, PMI will continue to support routine net distribution through ANCs (1.3 million nets) and to children under five through Expanded Program on Immunization clinics (0.6 million nets) to meet the national needs through these systems. PMI's support for net distribution for these two systems starts with the port of entry and continues through the provincial level down to the districts through a temporary, semi-parallel system. This will ensure increased accountability for the LLINs procured with PMI funding. Lastly, PMI will help strengthen the system of the government agency responsible for net distribution through supervision and auditing. Once the system is sufficiently strengthened and the NMCP demonstrates the capacity to manage the system, net distribution responsibilities will be transferred back to the government. PMI's coverage of ANC and Expanded Program on Immunization net needs will complement the mass universal coverage campaigns that are expected to be completed, nationwide, by the end of 2014 in all areas not targeted for IRS.

Indoor residual spraying: Indoor residual spraying remains a high priority vector control intervention for MISAU in Mozambique. Over the past several months, the GoM has been working on its first Integrated Malaria Vector Control Strategy, which is currently in draft form. This strategy highlights how best to implement malaria vector control interventions (LLINs, IRS, and larviciding) in a complementary manner. During the development of the Global Fund Round 9 Phase 2 proposal, the criteria outlined in this strategy was used to develop a list of 34 districts nationwide that will be targeted for IRS beginning in 2014; the remainder of the country will rely on universal coverage with LLINs.

PMI supported IRS in six districts in Zambézia Province and in 2010 increased to eight. In 2012, PMI reduced its IRS operations from eight districts to six in Zambézia. In the six districts that were covered, PMI achieved a 92% coverage rate; covering approximately 537,000 structures and protecting approximately 2.7 million people. PMI's IRS program will continue to scale back in 2013, with coverage of only four districts in Zambézia, targeting approximately 360,000 structures and 1.7 million people. In 2013, in line with the draft vector control strategy, PMI will continue enhanced epidemiologic surveillance, in addition to entomologic surveillance, in the four districts that have been phased out of IRS in 2012 and 2013 (Maganja da Costa, Mopeia, Nicoadala, and Namacurra), which will receive universal coverage net campaigns instead. This epidemiologic and entomologic surveillance will also take place in the four districts where PMI is conducting IRS operations.

PMI's support to IRS with FY 2014 funding is in line with the draft vector control strategy. PMI aims to implement targeted spraying in the four districts selected for IRS in Zambézia Province, where PMI has been implementing IRS since 2007. Zambézia Province continues to have the highest prevalence of malaria in Mozambique as shown in the 2011 DHS, necessitating continued investment in this province. In addition, PMI proposes to support targeted spraying in two additional districts in Zambézia Province, Morrumbala and Milange, if the net universal campaigns scheduled for early in 2014 do not occur. PMI's support will include procurement of personal protective equipment and IRS supplies, environmental monitoring, training, and supervision, with the target of covering approximately 270,000 houses total. PMI will again rely on the GoM to provide insecticide for the spray campaign. In addition, PMI will support ongoing epidemiologic and entomologic monitoring in all six districts. FY 2014 will represent a transition year for Zambézia as PMI will begin to decrease its operational footprint for IRS in the province, while at the same time expanding its IRS support outside of the province. Given the widespread geographic coverage of the national IRS program implemented by MISAU and concerns surrounding its quality, PMI, with FY 2014 funding, will begin to assist the GoM in strengthening the national spray program through cascade trainings and supervision of spray operations.

Malaria in pregnancy: According to data from the 2011 DHS, Mozambique has made relatively little progress on scaling up IPTp, with only 18.6% of women having received two or more doses of IPTp during their last pregnancy in 2011, compared to 16.2% in the 2007 MIS. The reasons for Mozambique's low coverage have not been confirmed, but are thought to be due to a combination of factors, including inconsistent stocks of sulfadoxine pyrimethamine (SP), lack of clearly articulated guidelines on the administration of IPTp, and lack of supervision, together with poor reporting practices. Due to the poor reporting of this intervention, it is believed that a high percentage of women that receive IPTp are not recorded, making the coverage of this intervention artificially low. In the past 12 months, PMI contributed to the creation and rollout of new registers for the Maternal & Child Health Program, which contained malaria specific indicators to help ameliorate this problem. In addition, PMI has been actively working to strengthen Mozambique's IPTp activities through stronger collaboration with the Maternal & Child Health Department at MISAU for training and supervision of its maternal and child healthcare workers. In 2013, PMI funds supported the procurement of 7.7 million tablets of SP, enough to cover the nationwide need for IPTp. PMI also supports the procurement and distribution of nets through ANCs, which contributes to PMI's MIP goals.

By the end of this year, Mozambique is expected to adopt the updated WHO IPTp guidelines, which recommend monthly doses of SP beginning in the second trimester and lasting throughout the duration of the pregnancy. The adoption of these new guidelines is expected to result in a subsequent increase in the national SP needs in Mozambique.

With FY 2014 funding, PMI will continue to support the integrated training and supervision of ANC staff and health workers in the provision of MIP-related activities at the central level, in addition to the procurement of LLINs for distribution at ANCs nationwide. PMI will provide more focused support for provincial-level supervision of ANC workers in four targeted provinces, where PMI will have established a provincial-level supervision platform for a multitude of malaria interventions in addition to interventions to address malaria in pregnancy. PMI will also support identification of barriers to receiving IPTp through a Field Epidemiology & Laboratory Training Program study and through the joint 2014 National HIV/AIDS Indicator Survey/MIS, and will procure approximately 10 million tablets of SP (approximately 3.3 million treatments) with FY 2014 funding to meet the expected elevated national demand, as the country implements the updated WHO IPTp guidelines. In addition, promotion of interventions to address malaria in pregnancy will continue to be emphasized in BCC activities through various platforms.

Malaria diagnosis: RDTs were introduced in Mozambique in 2007 and rolled out nationally in 2010; however, chronic issues, including lack of consumption-based distribution plans, poor warehousing and storage practices and inadequate logistics management, over the past several years have hampered efforts to improve malaria case management activities.

Over the past 12 months, PMI procured approximately 10 million RDTs, along with other laboratory supplies. The RDTs procured by PMI are distributed to all levels of the health system, including to community health workers (*Agentes Polivalentes Elementares da Saúde* or APEs) through kits. During the past year, more than 1,488 new APEs were trained nationwide, bringing the total number of APEs to 2,726. From May 2012 to April 2013, the APEs identified about

88,000 cases of malaria using RDTs. PMI is also supporting the training and supervision of laboratory staff, including those at the reference laboratory.

With FY 2014 funds, PMI will support the continued strengthening of diagnostic laboratories at all levels through procurement of necessary commodities, refresher training, supervision, and quality control of diagnostic testing. Included among PMI's activities will be the procurement of approximately 11.3 million RDTs to help fill the nationwide gap. In addition, PMI will continue to provide diagnostic supplies for the National Reference Laboratory for Blood Parasites, and will support training and supervision of laboratory staff in malaria diagnosis, use of RDTs, and quality assurance. PMI will continue its decentralized support that begins with FY 2013 funds by supporting the supervision of malaria diagnosis and case management activities through non-governmental organizations at the provincial level in four targeted provinces. PMI will also select two districts in each of these four provinces where supervision of APEs will be supported and lessons learned from these districts will be used to scale up this activity. In addition to the provincial-level supervision support of APEs, PMI will also continue to support the kitting of RDTs and ACTs for use by APEs, good program coordination at the central level, and strengthened data collection, training, and supervision aspects of the APE system.

Malaria treatment: Artemether-lumefantrine (AL) has been the first-line treatment for uncomplicated malaria in Mozambique since 2009. PMI has contributed significantly to covering Mozambique's national annual AL needs since PMI began and this will continue in 2013 with the procurement of approximately 11.2 million treatments.

The APE program is an important component of Mozambique's malaria case management plan. APEs serve as the first line of defense against malaria for people living in rural Mozambique, and for many people are the only opportunity to receive proper diagnosis and treatment for malaria. PMI's support for the APE program has focused on the provision of RDTs and ACTs for the kits used by APEs for community case management. In addition to the procurement of AL, PMI also continued to support refresher training of 2,356 clinicians in eight provinces in malaria case management over the past 12 months. Despite this progress, ensuring regular supervision of health staff has been a challenge.

With FY 2014 funds, PMI will procure approximately 4.4 million AL treatments, which in addition to contributions from the Global Fund, is expected to meet the national needs for 2015. PMI will also continue to strengthen the capacity of MISAU's supply chain management system to forecast and manage antimalarial drugs through improved logistics management capacity, with a focus on the distribution of AL through the kit system. With FY 2014 funds, PMI will support ongoing continued assessments of warehousing inventory management, as well as strengthening storage and distribution capability at the central level. PMI will also support the supervision of clinical staff in malaria case management at the central level, as well as at the provincial level in four target provinces through the new decentralized supervisory platform.

Behavior change communication: In the past 12 months, PMI and other partners supported the completion and approval of the strategic plan for malaria BCC, which provides an important framework for the implementation of all malaria BCC activities in country. The objective of the NMCP's BCC activities is to ensure that by 2016, 100% of the population is covered by key messages related to malaria prevention, diagnosis, and treatment. PMI has supported malaria BCC activities largely through the Inter-Religious Campaign Against Malaria (PIRCOM), a consortium of religious groups working in Zambézia, Nampula, Sofala, Inhambane and Gaza Provinces, in addition to limited central-level support.

With FY 2014 funding, PMI will continue to support PIRCOM's dissemination of key malaria messages through religious leaders and volunteers in five provinces. To expand the support beyond the provinces covered by PIRCOM, PMI will identify community-based organizations at the provincial level to implement both facility-based and community-based BCC activities. In this expansion, PMI will prioritize those provinces and districts with existing partners funded through the President's Emergency Plan for AIDS Relief (PEPFAR) or other mechanisms, in order to leverage funds and increase the efficiency of the interventions. Community-based BCC messages will include an explicit focus on MIP to encourage uptake of IPTp. With FY 2014 funding, PMI will continue to work in collaboration with U.S. Agency for International Development strategic information and health promotion colleagues to devise an M&E plan for the malaria BCC activities, including an assessment of the effectiveness of BCC interventions. Finally, PMI will continue to support MISAU's central level BCC activities, disseminate the new malaria communication strategy and strengthen the ability of the health promotion department to develop, implement, and coordinate BCC strategies and approaches.

Monitoring and evaluation: In 2012, the NMCP finalized its 2012-2016 M&E Plan, which is aimed at integrating a variety of M&E needs of priority health programs. In an effort to help strengthen Mozambique's M&E system, PMI supported the establishment of a temporary routine malaria data collection database from outpatient registers to allow for the routine collection of key malaria indicators. PMI's support for M&E activities over the past 12 months has been comprehensive and includes enhanced epidemiologic surveillance in Zambézia Province, collection of entomologic data in various sentinel sites to support the government's IRS program, support for health facility surveys of malaria commodity availability, and provincial-level support for M&E supervision. In addition, PMI will complete a joint MIS/National HIV/AIDS Indicator Survey in 2014. The PMI team will explore opportunities to include questions on IPTp in the 2014 survey to help determine the barriers for uptake. PMI's M&E support is complementary to other partners, including Village Reach and the United Nations Children's Fund (UNICEF), which are gathering critical data from APEs on malaria treatment, diagnosis, and commodity usage with support from the U.S. Agency for International Development's non-PMI health funds. PMI used data collected by Village Reach showing widespread stockouts of key malaria commodities from 2012-2013 to inform its decision to decentralize its support and focus on the lower levels of the health system to ensure the appropriate commodities are reaching their intended targets. The data also helped guide PMI's decision to support supervision of APEs in selected provinces.

Many of these critical M&E activities will be continued with FY 2014 funds, including support for expanded entomologic monitoring nationwide; the implementation of the health facility commodity surveys; M&E supervision from the provincial level to health facilities; the Field Epidemiology & Laboratory Training Program; and support for increased entomological and epidemiological monitoring in current or former PMI-supported IRS districts (*see IRS section*).

Capacity building and health system strengthening: PMI is committed to implementing the core GHI principle of health systems strengthening through support to capacity building efforts at all levels in Mozambique. Over the past 12 months, PMI has provided technical and programmatic support to the NMCP on a range of issues, including the M&E Plan, the draft Integrated Malaria Vector Control Strategy, the Malaria Acceleration Plan, the Global Fund Round 9 Phase 2 proposal, and other key policy documents. PMI has provided extensive support to build the entomological capacity nationally, in addition to the establishment of a provincial entomology laboratory and insectary in Cabo Delgado, which is staffed by provincial health department personnel through PMI support.

With FY 2014 funding, PMI will continue to decentralize its health systems strengthening support to provincial, district, and sub-district levels to help improve the quality of activities and to achieve greater impact, particularly with respect to LLIN distribution to ANCs and EPI, case management supervision, BCC implementation, and M&E supervision through provincial-level platforms.

STRATEGY

INTRODUCTION

President's Malaria Initiative

The President's Malaria Initiative (PMI) is a core component of the Global Health Initiative (GHI), along with HIV/AIDS, and tuberculosis. PMI was launched in June 2005 as a 5-year, $1.2 billion initiative to rapidly scale up malaria prevention and treatment interventions and reduce malaria-related mortality by 50% in 15 high-burden countries in sub-Saharan Africa. With passage of the 2008 Lantos-Hyde Act, funding for PMI was extended and, as part of GHI, the goal of the PMI was adjusted to reduce malaria-related mortality by 70% in the original 15 countries by the end of 2015. This will be achieved by continuing to scale up coverage of the most vulnerable groups — children under five years of age and pregnant women — with proven preventive and therapeutic interventions, including artemisinin-based combination therapies (ACTs), insecticide-treated nets (ITNs), intermittent preventive treatment of pregnant women (IPTp), and indoor residual spraying (IRS).

Mozambique was selected as a PMI country in FY 2007. This FY 2014 Malaria Operational Plan presents a detailed implementation plan for Mozambique, based on the PMI Multi-Year Strategy and Plan and the National Malaria Control Program's (NMCP's) 5-Year Strategy. It was developed in consultation with the NMCP, with participation of national and international partners involved with malaria prevention and control in the country. The activities that PMI is proposing to support fit in well with the National Malaria Control Strategy and Plan and build on investments made by PMI and other partners to improve and expand malaria-related services, including the Global Fund to Fight AIDS, Tuberculosis, and Malaria (Global Fund) malaria grants. This document briefly reviews the current status of malaria control policies and interventions in Mozambique, describes progress to date, identifies challenges and unmet needs if the targets of the NMCP and PMI are to be achieved, and provides a description of planned FY 2014 activities.

MALARIA SITUATION IN MOZAMBIQUE

Malaria is endemic throughout Mozambique, and its entire estimated population of 24 million people is at risk of malaria. Most of the country has year-round malaria transmission with a seasonal peak during the rainy season, from December to April. In addition, Mozambique is prone to natural disasters such as drought, cyclones, and floods, which may have contributed to increases in malaria transmission in recent years, particularly in low-lying coastal areas and along major rivers.

Malaria is considered the most important public health problem in Mozambique and accounts for 29% of all deaths, followed closely by AIDS at 27%. Among children less than five years old, malaria accounts for 42% of the deaths, followed by AIDS at 13%. *Plasmodium falciparum* accounts for 90% of all malaria infections, with *P. malariae* and *P. ovale* responsible for about 9% and 1%, respectively.

The recent 2011 Demographic and Health Survey (DHS) data show that malaria prevalence, using rapid diagnostic tests (RDTs), varies from 1.5% in the capital, Maputo, to 54.8% in Zambézia Province. Prevalence rates are generally higher in the northern region, varying from 43.3% to 52.1%, and lower in the southern region, varying from 1.5% to 36.8%. In the central region, the prevalence varies from 30% to 37%, except for Zambézia with 54.8% (*Figure 1*). The prevalence in rural areas is almost three times as high as the prevalence in urban areas, 46% versus 16%, respectively. Because of microscopy issues during the 2011 DHS, this Malaria Operational Plan (MOP) presents RDT rates as they are believed to be a more accurate representation of the malaria prevalence. The major vectors in Mozambique are *Anopheles gambiae* s.s., *A. arabiensis*, *A. funestus* s.l., and *A. funestus* s.s. Of the major subspecies of the *A. gambiae* complex, *A. arabiensis* is more prevalent in the south and *A. gambiae* in the north.

Figure 1. Malaria prevalence rates as estimated by RDTs, 2011

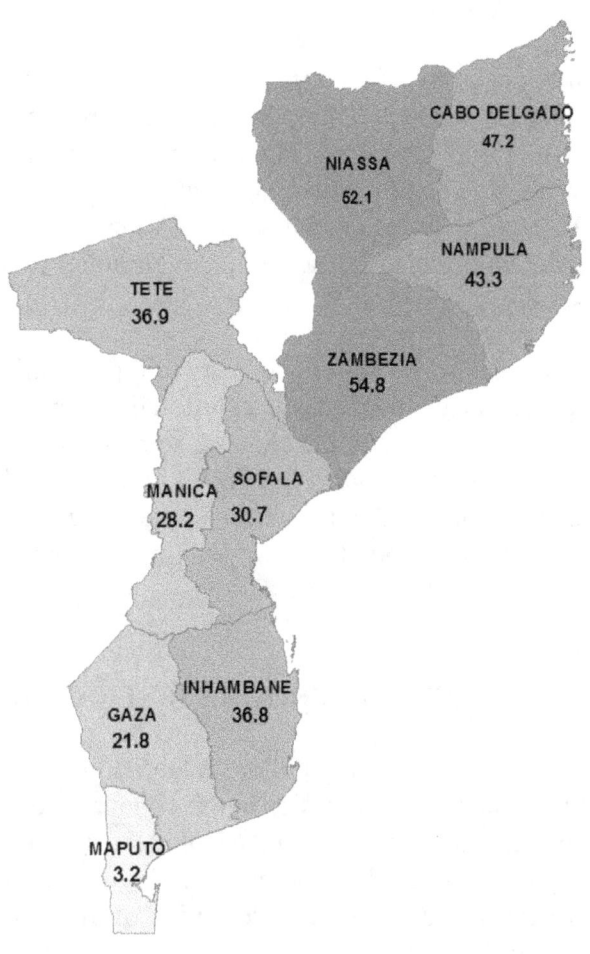

Source: 2011 DHS

HEALTH SYSTEM DELIVERY

In Mozambique, the public sector–the National Health Service (NHS)–dominates health service delivery. Although there is a growing private sector, it is largely limited to major cities. The public sector reaches an estimated 60% of the population.

The National Health Service consists of four levels. Level I includes both rural and urban health centers and health posts. These health facilities provide a package of primary health care services, have very limited laboratory capacity, and usually have a maternity ward but do not provide inpatient services. According to a 2004 World Bank Report, Level I facilities represent at least 40% of all health services and are typically the first (and often only) point of contact with the health system for a large portion of the population. Level II includes district and rural hospitals that offer diagnostic, surgical, and obstetric services and have general medical doctors on their staff. Level III consists of provincial hospitals, which offer curative services, have diagnostic services/equipment, and are training centers. Finally, Level IV is made of the country's three referral hospitals in Maputo, Beira, and Nampula, serving the southern, central, and northern regions respectively.

Recognizing the limitations of the National Health Service and the lack of professionally trained health workers, the country, with USG support, has begun revitalizing the community health worker program, which employs health workers known as *Agentes Polivalentes Elementares da Saúde* (APE). The APEs provide preventive and basic curative services, including malaria diagnosis (using RDTs) and treatment (with ACTs). A number of national and international nongovernmental organizations also work within the National Health Service to assist in the provision of health services.

Malaria control in the public health system consists of three administrative levels: central, provincial, and district. At the central level is a National Malaria Control Program (NMCP), although it is understaffed and some of the existing staff lack the technical skills to adequately manage the program. Each province has a provincial malaria focal point who coordinates the implementation of malaria control activities at that level. Recently, MISAU approved the creation of a district malaria focal point as a way to improve data management and reporting for malaria at that level.

NATIONAL MALARIA CONTROL PROGRAM STRATEGY AND ACTIVITIES

The NMCP is responsible for developing policy; establishing norms; and planning, organizing, and coordinating all malaria control activities in the country. Additional responsibilities include periodic assessment of the impact of malaria control activities, development of training materials on malaria case management for health workers at all levels, mobilization of domestic and external funds for malaria control activities, promotion of malaria awareness and advocacy, and leading operational research.

In 2012, the NMCP finalized the National Malaria Policy and the 2012-2016 National Malaria Prevention and Control Strategic Plan. The strategic plan focuses on continuing national-level scale-up of five objectives for malaria prevention and control:

1. Decentralization of malaria control activities, with 100% of districts in 2014 having malaria management capacity in place.

2. Access to at least one prevention method for 100% of the population by 2014.

3. Confirmatory laboratory testing on 100% of suspected cases of malaria throughout the entire health system, including APEs by 2014.

4. Malaria prevention messaging reaching 100% of the population by 2016.

5. Strengthened monitoring and evaluation (M&E) system so that by 2014 all districts are capable of reporting key malaria related indicators.

INTEGRATION, COLLABORATION, AND COORDINATION

Integrated health activities

Within the USG, the U.S. Agency for International Development (USAID) Mozambique Health Team has merged into one Integrated Health Office, maximizing the programmatic synergies among the President's Emergency Plan for AIDS Relief (PEPFAR), PMI, and other health programs. This change enhances administrative and technical efficiencies and avoids duplication of efforts, as well as facilitates a broader health systems approach across all USG programs, including maternal and child health (MCH), reproductive health/family planning, tuberculosis, HIV, malaria, and nutrition. An example of integration of USAID's health projects is a project PMI is supporting jointly with funds from MCH, reproductive health, family planning, and PEPFAR: integrated MCH services. This project, in line with Mozambique's GHI strategy, aims to strengthen antenatal clinic (ANC) services nationwide through support at the central level for guideline and training material development and quality of care improvement through "Model Maternities" and supervision. PMI supports the malaria in pregnancy (MIP) component of the project, which also receives MCH and PEPFAR funds. The merger has not been without challenges (time management for meetings, expectations of roles and responsibilities, and clear communication channels), but overall the merger has been successful in breaking down some of the vertical barriers, in line with GHI guidance.

Other examples of integration are in strengthening the supply chain management and improving laboratory diagnosis through microscopy. PMI, PEPFAR, and family planning staff leverage their resources to strengthen the capacity of MISAU's supply chain management system/Central Medical Stores (CMAM) and improve the supply chain at different levels. In microscopy, PMI and tuberculosis funding has been used for training and supervision, quality assurance, and procurement of laboratory supplies, to improve laboratory diagnosis of both malaria and tuberculosis.

Collaboration and Coordination

The Global Fund Round 9 Phase 2 proposal was written with direct input from PMI; activities and funding were tailored so that an activity not funded by one donor was supported by the other. An example of this distribution of activities is long-lasting insecticide-treated net (LLIN) coverage: PMI supports procurement and distribution of LLINs through ANCs for pregnant women, and Global Fund supports the procurement and distribution of the LLINs for universal coverage. In addition, because of its flexibility, PMI has been able to schedule the arrival of its shipments of ACTs and RDTs based on the expected arrival of Global Fund– and World Bank–supported commodities. A malaria commodity working group now meets every month to discuss quantification, procurement, stock levels, and shipments of all malaria commodities.

In recent years, the private sector in Mozambique, especially with the extractive industries, has rapidly expanded. MISAU is in discussion with a number of companies to explore the potential of public-private partnerships, including a malaria bond initiative. Specifically, there is strong interest in revitalizing the Lubombo Spatial Development Initiative, which was a very successful tri-party (South Africa, Mozambique, and Swaziland) malaria control initiative implemented in Southern Mozambique between 2000 and 2009. The PMI team is working with NMCP and other departments of MISAU to support the engagement with the private sector. As a first step, PMI has proposed mapping current private sector engagement to identify gaps and opportunities for joint investment. PMI has engaged with private companies such as Vale, Rio Tinto, and Anadarko to identify areas of collaboration and determine how the USG can support the private sector as they engage with MISAU at various levels. By the end of FY 2014, PMI hopes to have identified concrete activities to be implemented jointly with the private sector and MISAU.

PMI GOALS, TARGETS AND INDICATORS

The goal of PMI is to reduce malaria-associated mortality by 70% compared to pre-initiative levels in the 15 original PMI countries and to reduce malaria-associated mortality by 50% in new countries added to PMI in FY 2010 and later. By the end of 2015, PMI will assist Mozambique to achieve the following targets in populations at risk for malaria:

- >90% of households with a pregnant woman and/or children under five will own at least one ITN;
- 85% of children under five will have slept under an ITN the previous night;
- 85% of pregnant women will have slept under an ITN the previous night;
- 85% of houses in geographic areas targeted for IRS will have been sprayed;
- 85% of pregnant women and children under five will have slept under an ITN the previous night or in a house that has been protected by IRS in the last 6 months;
- 85% of women who have completed a pregnancy in the last two years will have received two or more doses of intermittent preventive treatment (IPTp) during that pregnancy; and
- 85% of government health facilities have ACTs available for treatment of uncomplicated malaria.

PROGRESS ON COVERAGE

Data from the 2011 DHS provides the most up-to-date information on key malaria indicators. Data from this survey are compared with results from PMI's 2007 baseline Malaria Indicator Survey (MIS), the 2008 Multiple Indicator Cluster Survey (MICS), and the 2009 AIDS Indicator Survey (INSIDA) in the table below. Overall, ITN coverage rates improved significantly from

2007 through 2011. However, other indicators increased only slightly between the 2007 and 2011 surveys and for many indicators, coverage decreased between the 2008 MICS and the 2011 DHS.

The 2011 DHS data show the most significant improvement in ITN coverage when compared with the 2007 MIS. Specifically, the proportion of households with at least one ITN increased from 15.8% in 2007 to 51.4% in 2011; similarly the proportion of children under five and pregnant women who slept under an ITN the previous night increased from 6.7% and 15.7% in 2007, respectively, to 35.7% and 38.9%, in 2011. Given that the 2011 DHS captured only part of a nationwide universal coverage campaign for ITNs, these coverage rates are expected to have increased significantly by the next national survey in 2014. More modest gains were seen with the proportion of children less than five years old with fever in the last two weeks who received treatment with an ACT within 24 hours of onset of fever, which increased from 4.5% in 2007 to only 15.3% in 2011.

Despite the improvements in some indicators, all still remain well below target levels, and many indicators have shown relatively little progress. For example, the proportion of women who received two or more doses of IPTp during their last pregnancy during the last two years increased from 16.2% to only 18.6%. IPTp and use of ITNs by pregnant women continue to provide challenges in Mozambique, where a more targeted focus is necessary.

Malaria Indicators in Mozambique

Malaria Indicators	2007 MIS (%)	2008 MICS (%)	2009 INSIDA (%)	2011 DHS (%)
Proportion of households with at least one ITN	15.8	30.7	NA	51.4
Proportion of children less than five years old who slept under an ITN the previous night	6.7	22.8	NA	35.7
Proportion of children less than five years old who slept under a bed net the previous night	15.7	42.1	48.7	38.9
Proportion of pregnant women who slept under an ITN the previous night	7.3	NA	NA	34.3
Proportion of pregnant women who slept under a bed net the previous night	19.3	NA	42.1	36.5
Proportion of women who received two or more doses of IPTp during their last pregnancy in the last two years	16.2	43.1	33.0	18.6
Proportion of children less than five years old with fever in the last two weeks who received treatment with an antimalarial within 24 hours of onset of fever	17.6	22.7	NA	22.2
Proportion of children less than five years old with fever in the last two weeks who received treatment with an ACT within 24 hours of onset of fever	4.5	NA	NA	15.3

Parasite prevalence estimates for each province, based on RDT positivity, are compared between the 2007 MIS and the 2011 DHS in *Figure 2*. Overall, prevalence decreased in all provinces, with the largest decreases occurring in Nampula (31.9% decrease) and Cabo Delgado (23.6% decrease). In total, five of the eleven provinces had a greater than 10% decrease in parasite prevalence between 2007 and 2011, and only three provinces had decreases less than 5%. The substantial decreases in parasite prevalence suggests that more substantial gains in disease reduction can be seen as the coverage of key indicators improve.

Figure 2. Provincial level parasite prevalence estimates, based on RDTs

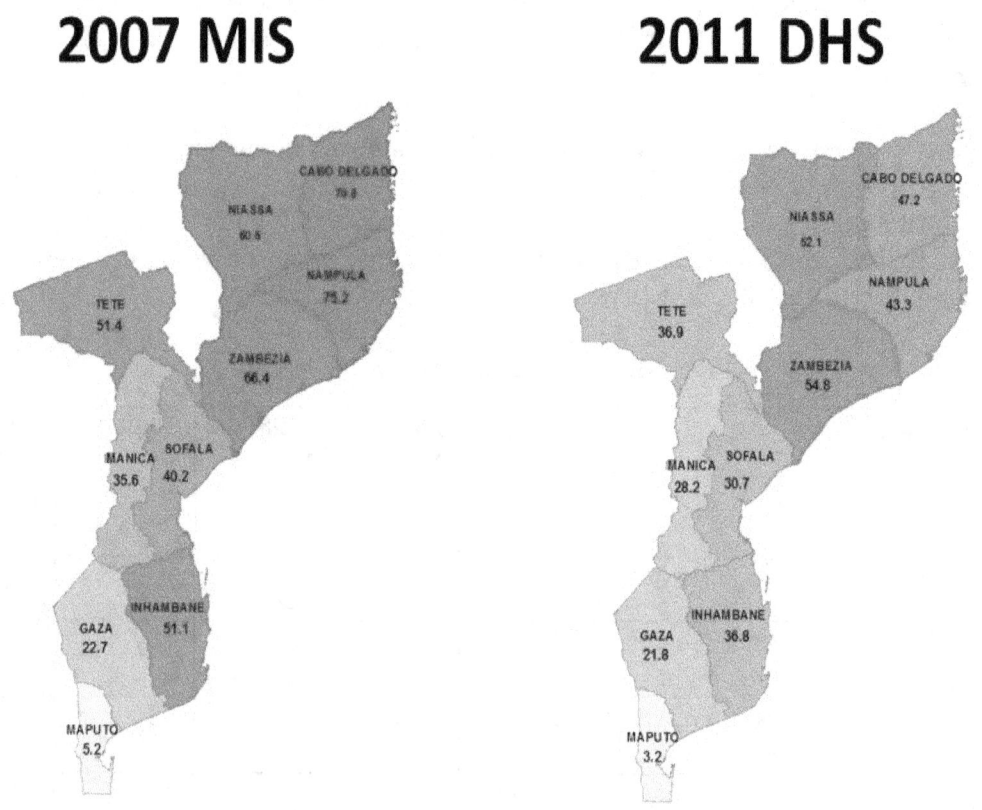

OTHER RELEVANT EVIDENCE ON PROGRESS

The results of two PMI-supported operational research projects are being prepared for publication in peer-reviewed journals after preliminary data were presented at scientific conferences. These projects focused on aspects related to the durability of LLINs and the mass distribution of LLINs through a universal coverage model developed in Mozambique.

The results of a prospective three-year follow-up evaluation of the LLINs that were distributed in Nampula Province in 2008 demonstrated a significant difference between polyethylene and polyester nets. The latter were found to perform better in terms of physical durability, in terms of holes in the LLINs, over the three years of follow-up. The results of this local evaluation may be used to inform LLIN procurements, in accordance with recent World Health Organization (WHO) guidance.

The results of a study of a universal LLIN coverage campaign conducted in Sofala Province in 2010 demonstrated high levels of coverage of household sleeping spaces and access to LLINs (80% and 85% respectively), which were maintained for a year after the campaign. A significant reduction in parasitemia (32%) among children under the age of five was also documented after one year. These findings give reassurance to the NMCP as it embarks on LLIN universal coverage campaigns throughout the country.

PMI launched the Roll Back Malaria impact evaluation process in collaboration with the NMCP in June 2013. The partners involved in the process have agreed on task assignments, and the draft analysis plan has been developed. The impact evaluation is expected to be finalized in mid-2014.

CHALLENGES, OPPORTUNITIES, AND THREATS

Challenges

The 2011 DHS results showed a slow pace of progress in scaling up malaria prevention and treatment interventions in Mozambique. Some problems that may have contributed to this slow progress include the frequent turnover of NMCP directors (five different directors in six years) and the lack of continuity in leadership and commitment from the NMCP and MISAU. Other challenges include shortages of appropriately educated and trained health professionals within malaria programs at the central, provincial, and district levels and high staff turnover.

Three major problem areas for malaria control in Mozambique are the optimal balance between ITNs and IRS for malaria vector control, the poor performance of the supply chain management system, and the weak M&E system. Supply chain issues are an ongoing challenge for all malaria commodities, but particularly for LLINs, as the country does not have a formal system for routine distribution. Leakage of commodities from the system in some provinces, particularly LLINs, has been reported. Mozambique is a large country with many remote areas and poor road conditions; many districts are not accessible during the rainy season. Information management systems to detect shortages and stockouts of malaria commodities need strengthening.

To address these challenges, PMI, in collaboration with other partners, is providing support at the central, provincial, and district levels to strengthen the supply chain and to improve M&E. PMI will support an evaluation of viable options for MISAU to take full responsibility of the supply chain system for LLINs. Meanwhile, and in order to ensure an increased accountability for the LLINs procured with USG funding, PMI will support a temporary, semi-parallel system, for net distribution from the port of entry to the provincial level and down to the districts nationwide. PMI is supporting the development of a vector control strategy and an insecticide resistance monitoring plan to guide vector control efforts in a coordinated, evidence-based manner. PMI is also shifting the focus of its support to malaria control efforts from the national level to the provincial level and below to achieve greater impact.

Implementation of behavior change communication (BCC) activities is also facing challenges. PMI has faced problems of poor performance of its implementing partners in this area, which was aggravated by the NMCP's weak technical capacity in BCC and poor coordination between the NMCP and the Health Promotion Department (DEPROS). The challenge of NMCP's coordination with DEPROS is not unique; other MISAU programs such as HIV/AIDS, tuberculosis, and MCH face the same challenges as well. One reason for this may be the lack of a clear mandate of DEPROS.

Opportunities

The GoM has reaffirmed its commitment to malaria prevention and control on several occasions, including during recent high-level visits from the Global Fund and PMI. In addition, President Guebuza recently assumed the role as chairperson of the African Leaders Malaria Alliance, which will provide an opportunity for Mozambique to share its successes in malaria control with other countries in the region and to learn from others' successes. The Minister of Health has agreed to meet monthly with the NMCP director and malaria partners to chart progress. The new NMCP director, who began in October 2012, has proved willing to seek advice, discuss issues, and consider different viewpoints, allowing for a fruitful collaboration with PMI.

The Global Fund has considered Mozambique one of the most under-funded countries and thus it is likely that under the new Global Fund funding model, Mozambique will be prioritized to receive considerable resources for malaria prevention and control. In addition, the relatively recent private sector boom in the extractive sector presents a strong opportunity for PMI to engage with the private sector to support malaria control goals.

The draft Integrated Malaria Vector Control Strategy (IMVCS) also presents a tremendous opportunity, as it lays out for the first time a clear vision of how various malaria control strategies will be employed in a complementary fashion. Finalizing this strategy and securing high-level approval will be essential in the coming year.

The recent approval of the strategic plan for malaria BCC offers an opportunity to boost the implementation of BCC activities at the central, provincial, district, and community levels. PMI will look into the possibility of using the vast network of community-based organizations funded through PEPFAR and other sources to include malaria BCC messages to increase the reach of these activities.

Threats

The major threat to malaria control is the uncertainty of funding. A Global Fund audit in December 2011 found that approximately $3.3 million in expenditures could not be accounted for. For this reason, Global Fund support was limited to commodity procurement and all direct funding to MISAU was stopped. The Global Fund required that the GoM reinvest this amount into the health sector as an additive investment to resolve the issue and allow Global Fund support to resume, which it did. The Global Fund is now considering resumption of direct support to MISAU through the Round 8 Health Systems Strengthening grant. However, other donors to PROSAUDE, Mozambique's common fund to support the health sector, are stopping disbursements to this fund. It is likely that some of these donors will consider direct support to provinces or project support, but it is uncertain whether malaria control will be their major priority.

Other threats are the possible emergence of resistance to insecticides and medicines. Insecticide resistance to pyrethroids has been well documented in southern Mozambique and in other sub-

Saharan African countries; it can have a devastating impact on the effectiveness of both IRS and LLINs. Antimalarial drug resistance to artemether-lumefantrine (AL) for *P. falciparum* infections has been well documented in Southeast Asia. This may be aggravated by the problem of sub-standard drugs infiltrating the market—a growing problem in some African countries.

PMI SUPPORT STRATEGY

PMI support to Mozambique is in line with the GoM's 2012-2016 National Malaria Control Strategy. Funding is targeted to fill gaps in activities not already supported by the NMCP, Global Fund, or other donors. PMI support is also targeted to translating best practices in malaria prevention and control to areas and activities currently supported by other funding agencies.

Supported activities continue to focus on achieving and maintaining high coverage of LLINs, particularly among the vulnerable populations of pregnant women and children under five, targeting IRS to complement national universal coverage campaigns, providing SP and support for IPTp scale-up, and improving case management, along with supportive activities such as BCC, strengthening supply chain management, and M&E.

PMI plans to decentralize its support to the provincial and district level, beginning with FY 2013 funding. The objective of this approach is to improve implementation of malaria-related activities through the facilitation of supervision, distribution of commodities, and M&E. PMI will establish a provincial-level platform for BCC, MIP interventions, M&E, and case management beginning with FY 2013 funding in four provinces (Nampula, Cabo Delgado, Zambézia, and a fourth yet-to-be-determined province). These provinces have been selected because of their high burden of malaria and the presence of strong local partners. In provinces where the USG has existing partners, efforts will be made to use these existing mechanisms, thereby following the GHI mandate and avoiding duplication of efforts. The activities that will fall under this effort to decentralize PMI support are the following: LLIN distribution to ANCs, IRS, case management supervision, BCC implementation, and M&E supervision.

OPERATIONAL PLAN

PREVENTION ACTIVITIES

Insecticide-Treated Nets

NMCP/PMI Objectives

The 2012-2016 National Malaria Control Strategic Plan set the ambitious target of covering 90% of the population with LLINs or IRS by 2014. Both the Malaria Acceleration Plan 2014-2016, which is a multi-year operational plan of the malaria control strategy, and the Global Fund Round 9 Phase 2 grant call for a scale-up of LLIN distribution and a more targeted approach for IRS. As a result, by the end of calendar year 2014, it is expected that more than 90% of the districts nationwide will have implemented a mass universal LLIN coverage campaign at least once since 2011, covering about 85% of the total population (Figure 3). These will include districts targeted for IRS in the past.

Figure 3. Map of Mozambique districts and years of universal LLIN coverage campaigns

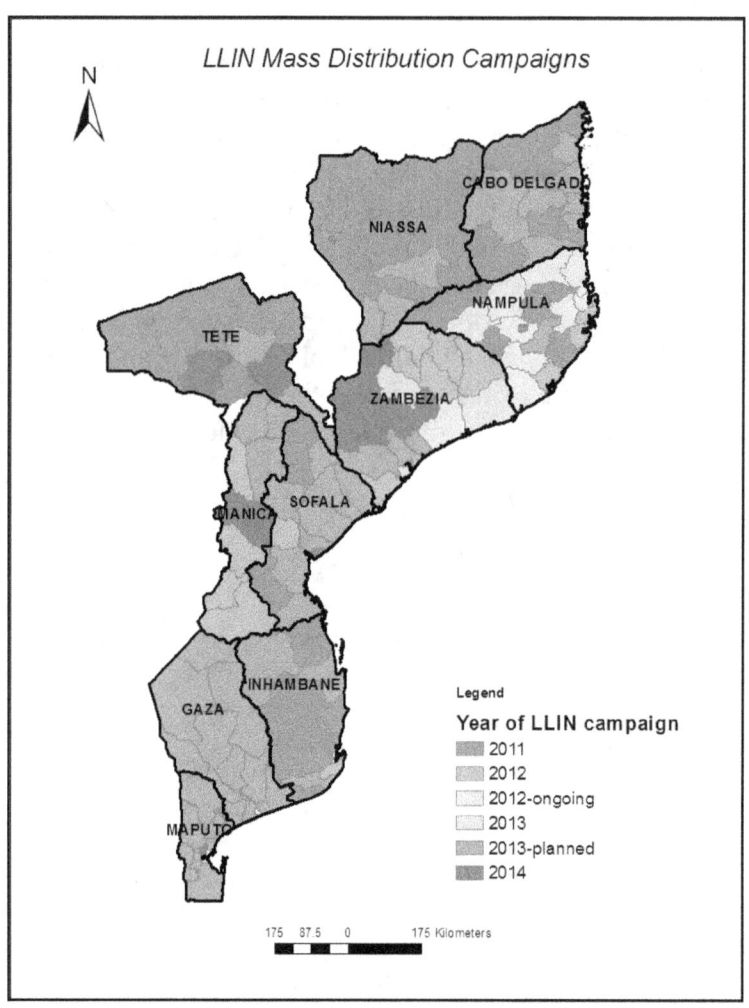

In keeping with the goals set forth in the Malaria Strategic Plan and the IMVCS, PMI aims to achieve the following objectives in the next five years:

1. Support MISAU's implementation of the IMVCS in a way that results in more than 90% of districts being covered with mass LLIN distribution campaigns;
2. Implement a temporary, semi-parallel supply chain to ensure routine distribution of LLINs to ANCs and through Expanded Program on Immunization (EPI) clinics to help maintain coverage of LLINs;
3. Support MISAU-led post-campaign surveys to ensure successful implementation and impact of mass distribution campaigns; and
4. Support the development and implementation of a national strategy for improving and sustaining LLIN coverage, which takes into consideration the specific needs of each province.

Progress since PMI was launched

Mozambique introduced free distribution of ITNs to children less than five years old and pregnant women as a national policy in 2006. Children less than five years old are reached through mass campaigns, while LLINs are delivered free of charge during ANC visits to pregnant women. In 2009, the country adopted the policy of universal coverage, defined as one LLIN for every two persons.

Since late 2009, PMI has focused its support on the purchase of LLINs for ANCs and their distribution to provincial warehouses throughout Mozambique. Although routine distribution of LLINs to pregnant women at ANC visits has been national policy since 2006, the system to support this activity has not been formalized; furthermore, PMI at present is the only donor providing funding for distribution of LLINs through routine systems. In 2011 a joint Global Fund/PMI Supply and Logistics Inventory Control Evaluation was performed to assess the weaknesses of the routine LLIN logistics system and provide specific recommendations for how to address them. The report called for the NMCP to work closely with PMI and other partners to develop a strategy and define a set of procedures for LLIN storage and distribution. Other recommendations included the need to improve the logistic information system and put in place measures to reduce commodity diversion. As a result, PMI-procured LLINs now carry bar codes that allow the implementing partner to track the product and identify the origin of "leaked" products. The PMI Mozambique team has also increased the branding of LLINs to ensure that the packages are appropriately marked to help prevent leakage. There has been documented leakage of ITNs in the past, most recently in a March 2011 investigation that identified the diversion of approximately 50,000 non-PMI nets from the public system. However, since then, there have been no documented leaks.

The implementation of mass universal coverage campaigns started in 2010 in 11 (out of a total of 144) districts; in 2011 universal coverage campaigns were carried out in 45 districts. During 2012, MISAU carried out Global Fund and World Bank-supported mass universal coverage campaigns in 21 districts, and in 2013, more than 5 million LLINs will be distributed through universal coverage campaigns in 61 districts.

Progress in the past 12 months

During the past year, PMI continued its support to routine distribution of LLINs to pregnant women, procuring approximately 1.3 million nets to meet the national needs through the ANC system. The Global Fund and World Bank provided complementary support to mass universal coverage campaigns as detailed above.

According to NMCP data, a total of 998,043 LLINs were distributed to pregnant women during the past year, representing about 77% of the estimated needs of this group. This low coverage was a result of a major stockout of LLINs caused by delays in shipments. In January 2012, MISAU introduced a new register at the prenatal consultation that can record LLIN consumption data, which is expected to greatly increase PMI's ability to ensure an appropriate supply. Preliminary data indicate that in 2012, 57% of the pregnant women attending their first ANC visit received an LLIN. This low coverage may be due to stockouts of LLINs, and under-reporting, due to unfamiliarity with the new register. In addition, pregnant women may receive an LLIN in a follow-up visit, which would not be reflected in this proportion.

To ensure that all pregnant women attending at least one ANC visit receive an LLIN, PMI continued to support a semi-parallel distribution system for LLINs, from port of entry to the districts in select provinces. In some provinces this support was extended to some health facilities.

In April 2013, PMI in collaboration with the NMCP organized a workshop on continuous distribution of LLINs and NetCALC, a tool used to predict LLIN needs. During this workshop, a draft national strategy for improving and sustaining LLIN coverage based on existing survey and campaign data was developed. Channels for consideration included ANC, EPI, schools, full-cost retail sales, and social marketing sales (to be targeted at urban and peri-urban communities). The strategy is currently in draft form and is expected to be completed by June 2014.

In 2014, MISAU is planning to procure and distribute 5.2 million LLINs through the Global Fund Round 9 Phase 2 proposal. The plan is to distribute these LLINs through mass universal coverage campaigns. However, the plan may be adjusted based on the recommendations to be defined in the national strategy for improving and sustaining LLIN coverage. PMI is planning to support post-campaign surveys of the national campaign in at least two districts.

Commodity gap analysis

The table below describes the LLIN gap analysis. Based on the draft national strategy for improving and sustaining LLIN coverage, Mozambique is planning to expand routine delivery in health facilities to include EPI distribution in calendar year 2015. Other continuous distribution channels are being considered, but as final decisions have not yet been made, they were not included in this gap analysis table.

Gap Analysis for LLINs, 2012-2016

Need	2012	2013	2014	2015	2016
Estimated population	23,700,715	24,366,112	25,041,922	25,718,054	26,412,441
Campaign target population[1]	7,900,238	8,122,037	8,347,307	8,572,676	8,804,138
Campaign replacement[2]	4,389,021	4,512,243	4,637,393	4,762,598	4,891,188
Routine ANC[3]	1,303,538	1,340,136	1,377,306	1,414,493	1,452,684
Routine EPI[4]				526,577	540,795
Total need	**5,692,561**	**5,852,379**	**6,014,699**	**6,703,672**	**6,884,671**
PMI (for ANC and EPI needs)	1,200,000	1,300,000	1,300,000	1,900,000	2,000,000
World Bank	1,400,000	2,029,886			
Global Fund	1,500,000	2,650,001	5,200,000		
Others	70,000		27,508	512,809	
Total nets distributed or committed	**4,170,000**	**5,979,887**	**6,527,508**	**2,412,809**	**2,000,000**
Gap	**1,522,561**	**-127,508**	**-512,809**	**4,290,863**	**4,884,671**

---

[1] Calculation based on 1/3 of total population per year.
[2] Calculation based on 1:1.8 net ratio.
[3] Based on assumption of 5.5% pregnancy rate.
[4] Based on existing population data for children under five years.

Plans and Justification

With FY 2014 funding, PMI will support routine ANC and EPI clinic distribution of LLINs from port-of-entry down to the district level nationwide using a semi-parallel supply chain system. Each district will have the responsibility of ensuring that health facilities receive a regular supply of LLINs. The expansion to include net distribution through EPI clinics was recommended to the team by the interagency PMI HQ team that discussed Mozambique's net strategy in March of 2013 as a way to ensure that all vulnerable populations are reached with nets. The NMCP and the United Nations Children's Fund (UNICEF) were also considering this approach so there was agreement at the country level to add this to our routine net distribution activities. A temporary semi-parallel supply chain system for routine net distribution is needed due to the dysfunctional nature of the government's supply chain system for nets. Nets, unlike RDTs and ACTs, do not fall under the essential medicines system managed by CMAM, which has benefited from significant supply chain strengthening efforts by USG donors in recent years. The system is considered temporary because the Mozambique team hopes to transition to a government-run system once it has been sufficiently strengthened and has the ability to take on this activity.

A key piece of Mozambique's future continuous distribution strategy may be school-based distribution as this channel could distribute, through students, about 40% of total number of LLINs needed each year. UNICEF is planning to collaborate with Global Fund to pilot school-based distribution of nets in 2014. Mozambique, which does not have experience with school-based distribution, will have the benefit of lessons learned from this pilot, as it plans for school-based distribution in calendar year 2015 after necessary consultative, coordination, and planning meetings. PMI will work with NMCP and other stakeholders to finalize the national strategy for improving and sustaining LLIN coverage, including the estimation of needs and the geographic areas to be targeted.

In addition to the procurement and distribution of nets, PMI will focus on strengthening the national system for routine net distribution through supervision and auditing so that net distribution responsibilities can be transferred back to the government once the system has been sufficiently strengthened. This will include supporting *Centro de Abastecimento*, the institution within MISAU responsible for managing nonmedical commodities. PMI will also provide support to improve the availability of consumption data for LLINs.

To help ensure coverage for the sizable commodities gap for LLINs projected for 2015, the PMI team will support the NMCP in the preparation of its application to the Global Fund for the new funding mechanism. PMI will also continue to advocate with other donors such as the U.K.'s Department for International Development to help cover the projected gap for 2015 and beyond to help ensure universal coverage.

Proposed Activities with FY 2014 funding: ($8,380,800)

1. LLIN procurement: Approximately 1.9 million LLINs will be procured for routine distribution through ANCs and EPI clinics, assuming a cost per net of approximately $3.50 ($6,680,800);

2. Support ANC & EPI LLIN distribution to district level: Support for ANC & EPI LLIN distribution from port of entry to provincial level to all districts. This will include transportation, warehousing, quantification of needs, and support to information systems that will allow collection of data on LLIN rationing, consumption, and stock levels ($1,500,000); and

3. Support to *Centro de Abastecimentos*: Provide support to *Centro de Abastecimentos* to strengthen the distribution system of LLINs through supervision and auditing ($200,000).

Indoor Residual Spraying

NMCP/PMI Objectives

One of the objectives of the 2012-2016 Malaria Strategic Plan is to ensure that 90% of the population of Mozambique has access to at least one method of malaria prevention (IRS or LLINs) by 2014. IMVCS was developed to reorient and better coordinate vector control interventions. The draft IMVCS calls for a more targeted approach to IRS and lays out a number of criteria for selecting IRS areas (areas of high malaria burden, high economic interest, high population but not highly urbanized centers, cross-border areas as a contribution to malaria elimination in neighboring countries, and easy physical access). The criteria outlined in this strategy were used by the NMCP to develop a list of 34 districts nationwide that will be prioritized for IRS beginning in 2014. The specific areas and number of houses to be sprayed will be reviewed every three years, based on available epidemiologic and entomologic data. As part of the insecticide resistance management plan, the IMVCS also outlines a plan for the preemptive rotation of insecticides that are logistically and financially feasible for Mozambique. Insecticides are to be rotated every two years, and the specific selection of insecticides for a rotation cycle will be determined based on insecticide susceptibility data. However, both insecticide choice and rotation cycle may vary based on the results of annual resistance testing. In Maputo Province, where pyrethroid and carbamate insecticide resistance has been documented, DDT and organophosphate insecticides will be used. In areas of current documented pyrethroid resistance, rotations will include DDT and carbamates.

In keeping with the goals set forth in the Malaria Strategic Plan and the IMVCS, PMI aims to support the following goals in the next five years:

1. An integrated, evidence-based approach to IRS that results in a more cost-effective and efficient targeted strategy for the entire country.
2. Implementation and improvement of the IMVCS, based on continually collected data, in a way that results in an integrated approach to vector control in Mozambique.
3. Strengthening of the MISAU-led IRS program.

Progress since PMI was launched

PMI-supported IRS in Zambézia Province began in 2007. The insecticide selection and the timing of the spray cycle have been dictated by MISAU. Historically, IRS insecticides have been procured by MISAU for all spray operations in the country, with the southern provinces using DDT and carbamates, and the central and northern provinces using pyrethroids. The exception has been Zambézia Province, which up until 2009 also used DDT. For the 2011 campaign, PMI for the first time procured pyrethroid insecticides to be used in Zambézia Province. In 2010 and 2011 the PMI IRS campaign in Zambézia Province increased from six to eight districts (Maganja da Costa, Milange, Mocuba, Mopeia, Morrumbala, Nicoadala, Namacurra, and Quelimane), covering 70% of the population of those districts.

PMI-Supported IRS Activities, 2007-2013

	2007	2008	2009	2010	2011	2012	2013*
Number of Districts Sprayed	6	6	6	8	8	6	4
Insecticide Used	DDT & PYR	DDT & PYR	DDT & PYR	PYR	PYR	PYR	PYR
Number of Structures Sprayed	586,568	412,923	571,194	618,290	660,064	536,558	358,559
Coverage Rate	97%	95%	97%	99%	99%	92%	N/A
Population Protected	2,588,385	1,457,142	2,263,409	2,945,721	2,825,648	2,716,176	1,795,338

*Represents targets based on the draft 2013 IRS work plan.

Currently, there are three groups supporting IRS in Mozambique: PMI, Global Fund, and MISAU. PMI focuses on parts of Zambézia Province, and MISAU sprays a significant number of districts in the remaining provinces. For the 2011 IRS campaign, the United Kingdom Department for International Development through UNICEF provided one-time support for the MISAU IRS program in 39 districts, and three districts in Gaza were supported by Médicos do Mundo.

Progress in the past 12 months

In 2012, insecticides for the MISAU IRS activities that were being procured by the Global Fund not only arrived very late, but only 4.8% of the requested amount was supplied, resulting in the cancellation of the MISAU national IRS campaign. The rest of these insecticides arrived this year, part of which will be used for PMI's 2013 IRS campaign in Zambézia. With budget cuts to PMI's IRS budget in 2012, IRS operations were reduced in Zambézia from eight to six districts. The districts of Maganja da Costa and Mopeia, where IRS was withdrawn, will transition to universal LLIN coverage later this year; PMI is also supporting epidemiologic and entomologic surveillance in these areas to monitor the impact of the vector control transition.

The 2012 spray campaign, carried out from October 8 through December 17, used the pyrethroid deltamethrin (wettable granules), for five of the six districts. Alphacypermethrin, another pyrethroid, was left over from the 2011 campaign and used in Mocuba district. A total of 1,923 men and women were hired and trained as spray operators, team leaders, locality and district supervisors, coordinators, and warehouse keepers. Of the 585,299 targeted structures in the six districts (Milange, Mocuba, Morrumbala, Namacurra, Nicoadala and Quelimane), 536,558 were sprayed, representing 92% coverage of eligible structures. The total number of persons protected is estimated at 2,716,176, including 174,370 pregnant women and 501,522 children under five years of age.

WHO wall bioassays were conducted to determine the quality of the spraying and the insecticide residual efficacy in three villages, one in each of the districts of Mocuba, Nicoadala, and Morrumbala. They were conducted 24 hours post-spray, using susceptible *An. arabiensis* mosquitoes from the insectary colony at Quelimane, which showed 100% mortality to deltamethrin in Nicoadala and Morrumbala. Similar results were found with the alphacypermethrin-sprayed walls in Mocuba, indicating that the quality of the spray operation was adequate. Monthly bioassays were conducted beginning immediately after spraying and for five months thereafter. These bioassays showed 100% mortality two months post-spray, after which the residual efficacy decreased in Morrumbala and Mocuba to 85.6% and 89.4% respectively in January 2013, three months post-spray. In Nicoadala the efficacy was maintained for slightly longer at 98.8% mortality in January. The decline in efficacy continued in Morrumbala and Mocuba to 54.4% and 71.9% in March 2013 at five months post-spray. The decline in residual efficacy in Nicoadala was sharper at 48.1% mortality in March 2013. These results indicate that both deltamethrin and alphacypermethrin were effective for three to four months post-spraying.

To provide more consistent support for the entomology personnel and activities in Zambézia, an entomologist and an entomology technician were hired by PMI and based in Quelimane. The entomologist, originally hired by PMI at the central level to support the national entomology surveys, has successfully transitioned to a MISAU/NMCP entomology position, bringing NMCP's total staff to four persons. In addition, PMI continued to support entomologic strengthening at the central and provincial levels with training, supervision, and standardization of entomology techniques. PMI will also support an additional technician for the National Institute of Health (INS) reference entomology laboratory to assist in the processing of mosquito samples from the national entomology surveillance activities, including mosquito material from the Zambézia IRS activities. The NMCP completed the National Entomology Monitoring and Evaluation Plan for 2012–2016, which includes insecticide resistance and residual efficacy testing for the IRS and LLIN programs and vector bionomics at sentinel entomologic sites. The number of entomologic sentinel sites and activities in the provinces will be scaled up from 2012 through 2016.

In an effort to support data-driven decision-making for vector control interventions, PMI has been supporting enhanced surveillance in Zambézia Province since 2012. Two former IRS districts (Mopeia and Maganja da Costa) have transitioned from IRS to universal coverage of LLINs as their primary method of vector control, and careful monitoring is required to assess the outcome of this transition. PMI has begun conducting enhanced surveillance in the two "transition" districts, as well as in all six districts with continued IRS operations in 2012; two additional districts that have never received any IRS will also be included as comparison districts. This activity is intended to add to the new reporting system rolled out in mid-2012, by utilizing existing PMI staff at the provincial level in Zambézia to ensure that the health facilities in the enhanced surveillance districts have the necessary tools (data collection tools as well as RDTs and ACTs) to conduct the surveillance, rather than the province-level PMI staff conducting the surveillance. In this sense, it can be considered a passive rather than an active data collection system. PMI is also ensuring the flow of the data from the health facilities to the district focal points is occurring as expected, as well as assisting the malaria focal points in the oversight of data quality. Because this activity relies on the infrastructure of the new malaria reporting system, data collection did not begin until training for the new reporting system took place in January 2013. As such, data are currently unavailable to support decisions on vector control. Once available, the results of the enhanced surveillance will assist both PMI and the Provincial Health Department (DPS) to target IRS activities, inform decisions on the allocation of IRS and LLINs, as well as provide important data on the outcome of switching from one vector control intervention to another.

The 2013 PMI IRS campaign in Zambézia will be scaled back to four districts (Milange, Mocuba, Morrumbala, and Quelimane) due to funding constraints. It will be carried out with deltamethrin, a pyrethroid, beginning in October. The insecticide will be supplied to PMI by MISAU, which is procuring the national need for IRS insecticides with Global Fund support. The previous PMI IRS districts of Namacurra and Nicoadala will transition to universal LLIN coverage in 2013. The objective is to cover at least 85% of the approximately 358,559 eligible structures in the four selected districts. With the possibility of emerging insecticide resistance in Zambézia Province and the transition of certain IRS areas to universal LLIN coverage, epidemiologic and entomologic monitoring in IRS districts will be expanded. PMI will also support a national environmental impact assessment, which will allow PMI to expand its future support for the MISAU IRS program such as guidance on training, supervision, and entomologic monitoring to areas outside of Zambézia Province.

Plans and Justifications

PMI will support the eighth round of IRS in Zambézia, as funding permits, and in alignment with the IMVCS IRS plan for 2014. Of the 34 districts identified as target districts for IRS based on the IMVCS criteria, four districts are in Zambézia Province (Quelimane, Nicoadala, Mocuba and Mopeia). PMI will target smaller geographical areas within each of these districts based on population density per the IMVCS, with the exclusion of urban areas. The rest of the districts of Zambézia, including Milange and Morrumbala (sprayed in 2013), and urban areas not covered by IRS, will have received universal LLIN coverage by 2014. However, in the event that the LLIN campaigns are not carried out in Milange and Morrumbala, PMI will implement targeted IRS in these two districts. It is expected that improved epidemiologic and entomologic data collected in 2013 and 2014, as well as close collaboration with the NMCP, will guide targeted spraying for the 2014 campaign to maximize the limited funding to achieve greatest impact. PMI will use the insecticides procured by MISAU through the Global Fund.

Epidemiologic and entomologic surveillance will be undertaken in the four districts in which PMI will be implementing IRS in 2014, as well as the former IRS areas of Maganja da Costa, Milange, Morrumbala, and Namacurra. With the possibility of emerging insecticide resistance in Zambézia Province and the transition to universal LLIN coverage in other former IRS districts, entomologic monitoring in IRS districts will be intensified. Enhanced epidemiologic monitoring will be based on health facility surveillance and PMI will provide support to ensure the availability of tools to conduct the surveillance (e.g., reporting tools as well as a consistent supply of RDTs and ACTs from existing national stocks) and oversight to ensure the flow of quality data from health facilities to the district level and from there to the provincial level, where the data will be entered into a malaria database (*see Monitoring and Evaluation Section*).

PMI proposes supporting MISAU in their national IRS program by strengthening each district's capacity to manage IRS activities occurring in its district and by improving the quality of MISAU's IRS operations. PMI will assist with the IRS training of trainers in a cascade approach for the central level NMCP team, provincial malaria managers, and key malaria staff. These personnel will then be responsible for conducting the training of the spray operators in the provinces. PMI will also provide support for the supervision of the MISAU-led national campaign to help improve the quality of spray operations.

Proposed Activities with FY 2014 funding: *($3,600,000)*

1. IRS implementation in Zambézia Province: Continue to support entomologically and epidemiologically targeted IRS operations in alignment with the Malaria Strategic Plan and IMVCS in four districts (Mocuba, Mopeia, Nicoadala, and Quelimane), covering approximately 270,000 houses. The number of structures and population to be covered in the four districts for the 2014 IRS operations will be refined at a later date based on malaria transmission data in an effort to target areas where impact of IRS could be greatest. In addition, PMI will support targeted IRS in Milange and Morrumbala if the 2014 LLIN universal mass campaign for these areas does not take place. PMI-supported activities for 2014 IRS operations will include training, supervision, enhanced epidemiologic surveillance in current and former IRS districts, and environmental monitoring throughout the country in anticipation of supporting MISAU IRS activities ($2,700,000);

2. Purchase equipment and supplies for the IRS operations in four districts: Procure adequate quantities of personal protective equipment and spare parts for spray pumps, etc. (excluding insecticides) ($250,000);

3. Support of NMCP IRS activities for training of trainers through a cascade approach and supervision of IRS activities ($500,000); and

4. Support ongoing entomologic monitoring activities in the IRS districts of Mocuba, Mopeia, Nicoadala, and Quelimane. In addition, support for entomologic monitoring (such as insecticide resistance testing and vector species monitoring) in the four former IRS districts of Maganja da Costa, Milange, Morrumbala, and Namacurra as these districts transition to LLIN universal coverage ($150,000).

Malaria in Pregnancy

NMCP/PMI Objectives

Prevention of malaria in pregnant women, through the use of SP for IPTp and ITN distribution, has been promoted in Mozambique since 2006. The national malaria and reproductive health guidelines recommend oral quinine in the first trimester and ACTs in the second and third trimesters for women with uncomplicated malaria; however, specific drugs are not mentioned. In 2013, Mozambique is expected to adopt the updated WHO guidelines recommending monthly doses of SP during pregnancy at the beginning of the second trimester. The national guidelines also recommend supplementation with iron and folic acid during pregnancy, but they are not specific in terms of dose and duration, and are being revised in line with the new WHO guidelines on IPTp.

Although procurement of SP and LLINs for distribution through ANCs is supported by the NMCP and its partners, the implementation of MCH programs is managed by MISAU's MCH department, which is under the same National Directorate as the NMCP. Currently, there is no formal mechanism for coordination of MIP activities between the NMCP and MISAU's MCH department; however both entities have identified focal persons for MIP and these individuals work very closely together. The priority for the MISAU MCH program is the implementation of an "Integrated Reproductive Health/Maternal-Neonatal-Child Services Package." A key objective of both the NMCP and the MCH Department is to ensure that 85% of women who have completed a pregnancy in the last two years will have received two or more doses of IPTp during that pregnancy.

In alignment with GoM objectives, PMI aims to achieve the following objectives in the next five years:
1. Ensure point-of-care delivery of MCH services through provincial and district support of supervision and training of ANC health workers;
2. Support simplification of the delivery and reporting of SP uptake by pregnant women through the rollout of the new WHO guidelines and training in their implementation.

Progress since PMI was launched

The percentage of women who receive at least two doses of SP during pregnancy was estimated to be 16.2% by the 2007 MIS, and thus considerable attention has been paid to improving the coverage of this indicator. The primary vehicle for delivering this support has been the "Integrated Reproductive Health/Maternal-Neonatal-Child Services Package." The idea of an integrated package of services for MCH has been in existence in Mozambique since 2009, although the formal Integrated Package was not launched until 2012. PMI has contributed to this effort, along with other USAID funding sources, since FY 2009. The USG has supported the development of national policies, norms, and guidelines; conducted training on the integrated in-service training package; provided support for the improvement of the quality of care; and coordinated MCH partners under the leadership of MISAU.

Despite these investments, the 2011 DHS found that the percentage of women receiving at least two doses of SP during pregnancy was only 18.6%, despite the fact that 91% of women reported receiving ANC services at some point during their last pregnancy from a trained health professional. The reasons for the low coverage of SP are complex, but are thought to result primarily from lack of supervision of case management practices at ANC facilities, inconsistent stocks of SP resulting from national stockouts and poor management of the supply chain, and lack of clearly articulated guidelines on the administration of IPTp. In addition, it is thought that a high percentage of women that receive both IPTp and ITNs are not recorded, making the coverage of these interventions artificially low and emphasizing the need for better monitoring and reporting of MIP indicators at the health facility level. PMI and Global Fund support of MIP activities at the provincial level is expected to alleviate some of the issues mentioned above, as this support will include supervision of provincial-level stocks and distribution to district and facility levels. In addition, the rollout of the new MIP registers is also expected to alleviate some of these problems by helping health facilities better track and report stocks of SP.

Progress in the past 12 months

Along with the 2011 DHS data, routine health information data showed low IPTp and LLIN coverage for pregnant women. Since then, the MCH has undergone an internal reorganization, and changes in personnel have resulted in increased collaboration with the NMCP. With help from the NMCP and PMI, new registers for the MISAU MCH program were rolled out in early 2012. Although these registers represent progress in that they contained malaria-specific indicators such as numbers of IPTp doses and ITNs distributed, they did not collect biomarker data, and training for the use of the new registers did not cover all facilities in the country.

The anticipated adoption of the updated WHO guidelines on IPTp is expected to result in much simpler and easier-to-understand national guidelines on the administration of SP and a subsequent increase in IPTp uptake. The MCH program and the NMCP, with PMI support, have revised the ANC registers to reflect the new guidelines, as well as to incorporate malaria biomarker indicators. PMI has continued to support provision of ANC services to pregnant women through training and supervision. PMI also supplied 100% of the projected SP need for the country in 2013.

Plans and justification

As with the reprogrammed FY 2013 funds, MIP activities supported with FY 2014 funds will be focused at the provincial level and below through placement of PMI-supported personnel in four key provinces: Cabo Delgado, Nampula, Zambézia, and a fourth yet-to-be-determined province. These personnel will provide on-the-ground mentoring, supervision, and support to DPS staff to ensure proper supervision and training is provided to ANC clinicians on case management of MIP, as well as on the collection and reporting of key MIP indicators.

PMI will also continue to provide support at the central level to the integrated supervision of health workers at ANCs. In addition, PMI will continue to support the rollout of the new WHO guidelines for SP, trainings for ANC health workers on implementation of the guidelines, and the rollout of new ANC registers that will collect malaria-specific indicators.

In anticipation of an increase in demand for SP resulting from the new WHO guidelines, PMI will procure approximately 10 million tablets of SP, more than the need predicted in the gap analysis below, as the gap analysis does not take into account the introduction of the new guidelines, which are expected to increase national SP needs dramatically. Because the demand for SP under the new WHO guidelines is uncertain at this point, PMI is prepared to reprogram FY 2014 funds once the actual need is known.

Gap Analysis for SP, 2013-2016*

	2013	2014	2015	2016
National SP needs (tablets)	7,730,988	5,774,662	6,556,250	7,374,158
Global Fund	-	-	-	-
World Bank	-	-	-	-
PMI	7,730,988			
Gap	0			

*Gap analysis was based on older guidelines of two doses of SP during pregnancy, and thus does not take into account increased needs resulting from the expected adoption of the updated WHO guidelines.

Proposed Activities with FY 2014 funding: ($900,000)

1. Support technical assistance for training and supervision of ANC staff in MIP. Central and limited provincial level support for integrated supervision of health care workers at ANC clinics, and rollout and training on new WHO guidelines on SP ($200,000);

2. Provincial-level support for training and supervision of ANC staff in MIP. Decentralized support for integrated in-service training and supervision of ANC health workers on prevention of MIP in four targeted provinces (Cabo Delgado, Nampula, Zambézia, and another yet-to-be named province) ($300,000); and

3. Procurement of SP. Procurement of approximately 10 million tablets of SP (3.3 million treatments) to meet national needs ($400,000).

CASE MANAGEMENT

Malaria Diagnosis

NMCP/PMI Objectives

According to Mozambique's updated national treatment guidelines, all patients suspected of having malaria must have a confirmatory diagnostic test before receiving treatment with an ACT. Due to difficulties involved in implementing and ensuring the presence of high-quality microscopy, RDTs are the preferred test for primary diagnosis of malaria. Microscopy is reserved for suspected treatment failures, severe febrile illness, and cases referred from lower levels of care. The NMCP and PMI prioritize the scaling up of quality-assured diagnostic testing at both the facility and community level through procurement of microscopes, laboratory supplies, and reagents; scaling up quality assurance systems for malaria microscopy and RDTs; and procurement of RDTs to be used at the facility and community level.

In line with the GoM objectives, PMI aims to achieve the following objectives in the next five years:

1. Strengthen supervision and training of malaria diagnosis at the provincial level and below through the implementation of provincial focal points for malaria case management.
2. Improve the forecasting, allocation, distribution, stock management, and use of RDTs in the country.
3. Implement a quality control/quality assurance program for both microscopy and RDTs.

Progress since PMI was launched

In support of the NMCP objectives, the National Reference Laboratory for Blood Parasites was refurbished, quality assurance testing practices have been developed, and supervision guidelines for malaria diagnosis have been completed. In addition, central and regional level training of microscopy trainers was performed, followed by the subsequent training of 95% of the existing laboratory staff in the country by these trainers.

Progress in the past 12 months

PMI continued to procure laboratory consumables used for quality control activities and training of staff. PMI supported the training of eight reference laboratory staff on malaria microscopy, including preparation of slides, slide reading, parasite density and standard operating procedures. The training was carried out at *Centro de Investigação em Saúde da Manhiça*, which has a laboratory with ISO certification for malaria. Despite the progress in trainings, poor supervision and lack of quality assurance measures have resulted in the overall poor quality of microscopic diagnosis of malaria, particularly below the provincial level. Moreover, stockouts of microscopy reagents such as Giemsa stain, methanol, and immersion oil are common, further hampering sustained progress in diagnostic capacity.

In 2013, PMI procured approximately ten million RDTs to help ensure the provision of appropriate case management. However, the roll out of RDTs is facing several challenges, including lack of consumption-based distribution plans, poor warehousing and storage practices, and poor logistics management. As a result, there have been reports of RDT stockouts at peripheral levels. Furthermore, at the time of writing, there were at least two different brands of RDTs circulating in the country, SD Bioline and First Response (both are single-species tests). These brands have different specifications in terms of number of drops and reading time, making it difficult for health workers to follow the specifications correctly. This may lead to errors and inconclusive results, which may affect the health workers' confidence in RDTs. To address these issues, a study protocol to assess the distribution and use of RDTs has been developed, and the award is pending. It is expected that the information collected through this study will be used to improve the allocation and distribution of RDTs, as well as highlight current challenges of RDT use and interpretation by health workers so that these can be adequately addressed during laboratory supervisory visits.

Plans and Justification

With FY 2014 funding, PMI will continue to strengthen INS capacity to implement quality assurance activities for malaria microscopy and RDTs. PMI will continue to support the scale-up of diagnostic testing for malaria by procuring more than 200 microscopes and ensuring a full supply of reagents to cover a year's worth of activities at 200 of the 254 health facilities performing microscopy. Prior to the purchase and distribution of new microscopes, an inventory of the existing supply of microscopes will be performed in 2013 to ensure the appropriate numbers are being purchased. PMI is actively engaging other donors to help fund this important area.

PMI will procure approximately 11.3 million RDTs, which will be delivered through various systems, including the APE kits. For additional information on PMI's case management-related support to the APE program, please see the *Treatment* section. PMI and Global Fund Round 9 Phase 2 will cover two-thirds of the country's needs, leaving a gap of approximately eleven million RDTs. Discussions with other donors to help meet this gap are ongoing. In order to address the challenges of having multiple RDT brands circulating in country, PMI will work with NMCP and Global Fund to assess the feasibility of having only one brand of RDT.

In the past two years, efforts have focused on training of both clinical and laboratory staff. With FY 2014 funds, PMI will support eight supervision visits by central level staff to four provinces (Cabo Delgado, Nampula, Zambézia, and another that has not been names); PMI will also ensure that at least 30 districts of the above mentioned provinces receive quarterly supervision visits.

Gap Analysis for RDTs, 2013-2016

	2013	2014	2015	2016
RDT National Needs	32,473,084	29,968,454	35,153,064	34,508,130
Global Fund Round 9 Phase 2	-	-	12,414,684	5,787,251
Global Fund Round 9 Phase 1	12,868,325	-	-	-
World Bank/Health Sector Development Plan/CMAM	8,600,000	-	-	-
PMI	9,956,375	16,400,000	11,300,000	-
Gap	1,048,384	13,568,454	11,438,380	28,720,879

Proposed Activities with FY 2014 funding: ($7,317,100)

PMI will support the continued strengthening of diagnostic laboratories at all levels through procurement of necessary commodities, refresher training, supervision, and quality control of diagnostic testing. The proposed activities are as follows:

1. Procure RDTs: Support will be provided to procure approximately 11.3 million single species RDTs ($7,000,000);

2. Support to National Reference Laboratory: Continue support to the INS National Reference Laboratory with procurement of microscopes, microscopy kits and reagents for routine reference activities, and repair parts for malaria-related diagnostic equipment ($50,000);

3. Support supervision of laboratory diagnosis: Provide supervision of laboratory staff in malaria laboratory diagnosis, use of RDTs and quality assurance ($250,000); and

4. Technical assistance from the U.S. Centers for Disease Control and Prevention (CDC): CDC staff to provide technical support and supplies needed to conduct training of NMCP personnel and INS laboratory strengthening activities ($17,100).

Malaria Treatment

NMCP/PMI Objectives

According to national guidelines updated in 2009, the first-line treatment of uncomplicated malaria is AL. Artesunate-amodiaquine is used as an alternative. The drug of choice for treatment of severe malaria is parenteral artesunate. Quinine remains the recommended treatment for pregnant women during their first trimester and for suspected failures to AL. Rectal artesunate is recommended for pre-referral treatment of severe malaria.

Given the limited reach of the National Health Service, which covers approximately 60% of the population, Mozambique launched a revitalization of the APE program in 2011. APEs provide 80% of rural communities' preventive care and 20% of their curative care, for illnesses such as upper respiratory tract infections, diarrheal diseases, and malaria. For malaria, APEs diagnose with RDTS and provide ACTs to those with positive test results. The APE program is an important component of Mozambique's malaria case management plan. They serve as the first-line of defense against malaria for people living in rural Mozambique, and for many residents, APEs are the only option for proper malaria diagnosis and treatment.

Ensuring that the entire population of the country has access to proper malaria treatment remains the goal of the NMCP, despite many challenges. In alignment with the GoM, PMI aims to achieve the following objectives in the next five years:
1. Strengthen malaria case management supervision and training at the provincial and district levels.
2. Support and expand community case management of malaria.
3. Strengthen warehousing, management, and supply chain for antimalarials.

Progress since PMI was launched

Since 2007, significant progress has been made to simplify and streamline national standards of care for malaria treatment. In 2011, national case management guidelines were finalized in line with WHO treatment guidelines for uncomplicated and severe malaria. Clinicians at all levels of the health system have been trained on the implementation of these guidelines in all eleven provinces, and central level support for the supervision of these activities has been ongoing for the past several years.

The APE program has been progressively scaled up since 2011. There are currently 2,726 trained APEs across the eleven provinces of Mozambique. This is in line with MISAU's plans to gradually roll out the revitalized program and has exceeded MISAU's target of 2,500 trained APEs by 2013. There is no current estimate of the number of APEs needed in the country to ensure sufficient coverage, although discussions are under way with USAID and several other donors and MISAU about plans to expand the APE program in the future. Partners, including Village Reach and UNICEF, are gathering critical data from APEs on malaria treatment, diagnosis, and commodity usage. Specifically, preliminary Village Reach data from December 2012 through April 2013 showed that while 50-80% of APEs were reporting consumption data in the two target districts, fewer than two-thirds of the APEs were receiving malaria commodities. In addition, APEs reporting stockouts of RDTs or one of the four presentations of AL ranged from an average of 27% to 63% over the course of those five months.

Progress in the past 12 months

PMI continued to support refresher training of clinical staff in malaria case management; 80% (2,356) of clinicians in eight provinces (Cabo Delgado, Inhambane, Manica, Maputo, Niassa, Sofala, Tete, and Zambézia) were trained. Support to the other provinces was provided by WHO. However, ensuring regular supervision of health staff has been a challenge and no supervision of health staff has been carried out in the past 12 months with PMI support due to a lack of training materials.

PMI continued to support the development of the Integrated Health Package, which includes activities related to prevention and treatment of malaria during pregnancy and management of malaria in children under five. This package is currently being tested and is expected to be finalized by the end of FY 2014. In line with its five-year goals, PMI has refocused its support for case management from the central level to the provincial and district levels.

During the past year, more than 1,488 new APEs were trained nationwide, bringing the total number of APEs to 2,726. From May 2012 to April 2013, APEs treated approximately 99,000 patients at the community level. This total includes 88,000 cases of malaria diagnosed using RDTs, while the remaining cases received a clinical diagnosis. Of these, 56% of cases were in children under the age of five years. Although PMI did not support the training of APEs, all RDTs and ACTs used in this program are purchased by either PMI or the Global Fund.

Plans and Justification

With FY 2014 funds, PMI will continue its efforts to strengthen the supply chain at all levels, with more focus at the provincial level. To coordinate the activities at the provincial level, PMI will recruit regional logistics advisors, one for the northern region (Niassa, Cabo Delgado and Nampula Provinces); one for Zambézia; and one for the central region (Tete, Manica and Sofala). The southern region (Maputo, Gaza and Inhambane) will receive support from Maputo.

PMI will procure approximately 4.4 million AL treatments, to be distributed through various platforms including APE kits. If the 11.5 million treatments of AL included in the Global Fund Round 9 Phase 2 proposal are procured, Mozambique will have a surplus of about five million treatments of AL. However, given the uncertainty of the Global Fund shipments, PMI will maintain its plan of procuring 4.4 million treatments of ACT, which can be reprogrammed at a later stage to procure more RDTs if needed. The needs for severe malaria treatments will be covered by PROSAUDE, donors, and the Global Fund.

PMI will continue its support of clinical oversight of case management activities of health staff, through supervision. Building on efforts that are expected to begin in late 2013, this support will be provided through nongovernmental organizations operating at the provincial level, instead of being the responsibility of central-level partners. These activities will be started with FY 2013 funds in selected districts of four provinces (Cabo Delgado, Nampula, Zambézia, and one province yet to be selected). PMI will also select two districts in each province where supervision of APEs will be supported. The lessons learned in these districts will be used to scale up this activity.

At the central level, PMI will provide technical assistance to improve the efficiency of the APE program's coordination, increase the overall quality of the program, and improve the existing M&E systems. In addition, PMI will continue to support MISAU's Training Department in the development and updating of training and supervision materials and will support provincial supervision visits to at least four provinces, twice yearly.

Gap Analysis for ACTs, 2013-2016

	2013	2014	2015	2016
AL National Needs	17,137,459	13,012,155	10,487,040	10,572,000
Global Fund Round 9 phase 2	-	-	11,643,843	2,938,080
Global Fund Round 9 Phase 1	933,888	-	-	-
WB/HSDP/CMAM	4,883,821	-	-	-
PMI	11,197,530	9,817,796	4,400,000	-
Gap	122,220	3,194,359	-5,556,803	7,633,920

Description and Budget for Proposed Activities with FY 2014 funding: ($5,700,000)

1. Procure ACTs: PMI will procure approximately 4.4 million AL treatments for the treatment of uncomplicated malaria ($4,000,000);

2. Provide technical assistance to strengthen the antimalarial supply chain and overall pharmaceutical management system of MISAU: Continue to support strengthening CMAM's capacity to forecast and manage antimalarial drugs through improved logistics management capacity, with particular support for AL distribution at the health facility and community levels. PMI will also support ongoing assessments of warehousing inventory management, as well as strengthening storage and distribution capability at the central level ($600,000);

3. Support warehousing and drug management: Building on achievements already made at the central level warehousing facilities (*see Pharmaceutical Management section*), PMI, along with PEPFAR, will support regional or provincial technical support to improve warehouse management, supervision of the Logistics Management Information System (LMIS), and transportation of medicines to strengthen peripheral-level capacity in selected provinces ($300,000);

4. Central supervision support: Facilitate and assist with planning and implementation of supervisory visits of central level staff to provinces, as well as technical support for malaria case management ($250,000);

5. Decentralized support of case management supervision: PMI will focus efforts to improve supervisory capacity for malaria case management in four targeted provinces (including Cabo Delgado, Nampula, Zambézia, and another province yet to be selected) through facilitation of the logistics aspects of supervision and assistance in supervisory planning ($300,000); and

6. Central support to APE coordination: PMI will provide technical assistance to improve the efficiency of the APE program's coordination, increase the overall quality of the program, and improve the existing M&E systems. PMI will continue to support MISAU's Training Department in the development and updating of training and supervision materials and will support provincial supervision visits to at least four provinces, twice yearly ($250,000).

Pharmaceutical Management

NMCP/PMI Objectives

Although access to essential health services throughout the country is low, MISAU remains committed to improving access and recognizes the need to invest in health system strengthening by focusing on three key areas: financial management systems, health management information systems and procurement, and supply management.

Central de Medicamentos e Artigos Médicos is the national entity with primary responsibility within MISAU for all central-level supply chain functions, including procurement of all pharmaceuticals and related health supplies. In collaboration with the NMCP, CMAM continues to manage forecasting needs and supervises the procurement, storage, and distribution of all essential medicines and related medical supplies, except ITNs, from the central level to the provincial warehouses.

Multiple factors have contributed to the dysfunctional supply chain and logistics system in Mozambique, including high turnover rates of personnel at both the NMCP and CMAM. Frequent changes to national-level diagnostic and treatment guidelines have also had a disruptive effect on the supply chain. Operationally, this has translated into expiry and the mismanagement of life-saving commodities. The ability of the GoM to facilitate the regular delivery of good-quality medicines and related commodities, including those for malaria, is a primary objective of MISAU, the NMCP and CMAM, as access to good quality medicines is a key factor in health services utilization.

The public health system in Mozambique has parallel logistics systems, one targeting only the health centers and APEs, each with a distinct kit of essential medicines, and a second system known as the *Via Classica,* which distributes to provincial-level depots. For the first system, kits are prepared overseas through the issuance of a biannual tender financed by pooled MISAU resources and other donor funds. The kits are then delivered to the four main ports: Maputo, Beira, Quelimane, and Nacala. The central medical stores at each port are bypassed and the kits are delivered straight to provincial warehouses. This is a push system down to the health facilities and APEs.

The second logistics system, the *Via Classica,* distributes medicines and commodities on a quarterly basis to the provincial depots. Kits are delivered to one of the two central warehouses in Maputo and a warehouse in Beira, which in turn supply the three central hospitals and ten provincial warehouses. Each of the ten provincial warehouses supply the district warehouses, rural hospitals, general hospitals, and provincial hospitals. Malaria drugs, including AL, are managed within this kit, and the system requires health facilities to report consumption data.

In addition to the two public distribution systems, there is also a separate PMI-supported ACT, and recently RDT, kitting system, initially developed in response to the bulkier Coartem® packaging. Currently, a PMI implementing partner supports this system, which is managed out of the central warehouse in Zimpeto. These malaria kits are distributed in parallel with the essential medicine kits and are distributed to both health facilities and APEs.

In alignment with the GoM, PMI aims to achieve the following objectives in the next five years:

1. Develop more effective public sector medical supplies/commodity procurement capacity.
2. Improve public sector warehousing and distribution at all levels.
3. Improve the use of medicines and develop more effective pharmaceutical services.
4. Strengthen the MISAU/Pharmacy Department's strategic planning and management capacity.
5. Strengthen overall regulatory capacity.

Progress since PMI was launched

To date, the USG has made significant contributions toward supply chain strengthening and pharmaceutical management in efforts to ensure access to good quality commodities as it relates to warehouse strengthening, especially in central-level warehousing. Several years ago, the main central warehouse, Zimpeto, located in the outskirts of Maputo, and the Beira regional warehouse in Sofala Province were refurbished. Together with another Maputo-based warehousing complex, Adil, these warehouses were to be linked to the Beira and Nacala warehouses to form a centrally managed, national system with accurate information on stock status for all essential commodities. However, refurbishment of the Nacala-based central warehouse has been slow to start. While the warehousing management information system is not yet operational in each of the regional warehouses (nor are refurbishments complete), both CMAM and the NMCP are supportive and recognize the need for a 'real-time' functional warehousing management system.

In the last six years, there have been three changes to the first-line treatment of uncomplicated malaria; a new first-line severe malaria treatment; the finalization of diagnostic guidelines; the roll-out of malaria RDTs on a national level; and the development of a supply chain master plan. Despite the problem with Mozambique's pharmaceutical management and supply chain system, good quality first-line ACTs are reaching the health facilities, and RDTs are being pushed out to the eleven provinces.

Through significant efforts on the part of CMAM, the NMCP, and USG donors, a computerized LMIS is now operational nationally in each province. This computer-based, real-time LMIS, called SIMAM, is an Access-based program and relatively easy to use; warehouse staff in all provinces, and centrally, have been trained. The original intent was for each district to also be linked to the SIMAM LMIS, but due to financial, human, and technical constraints, this has yet to happen.

Progress in the past 12 months

The Medicines Technical Working Group (*Grupo Tecnico do Medicamentos*) established several years ago through collaborative efforts of various USG implementing partners, has helped this past year to improve the management and oversight of health commodities. Specifically, the group formed eight sub-working groups, one for each of the eight major health commodities managed under CMAM. Quantifications and gap analyses for all medicines, including antimalarials, were conducted, in part as a response to the Global Fund's requirements for continued funds dispersal. While some of the groups are more effective than others, each continues to meet to review and adjust commodity pipelines and supply plans accordingly.

In spite of erratic ACT stock procurement and distribution, as well as cumbersome customs clearance processes that often delay the release of antimalarials, the PMI-financed ACT/RDT kitting system is proving effective, as evidenced by the growing number of kits pushed down to the provincial level, as well as by supporting data from the now functional End Use Verification activity, a tool used to assess the malaria-related commodity supply chain and the availability of malaria-related commodities at the health facility level.

While the PMI-funded commodity kits are a parallel system, they remain the one reliable mechanism to ensure ACTs and RDTs are moving through the public health system beyond the provincial level where they are needed most. RDTs were added last year, seeded with World Bank funds, but going forward PMI-financed RDTs will also be used in the kitting. From the time kitting began in 2009, almost 95,000 kits have been distributed down to both the APEs and health facility level.

As part of MISAU's commitment to improve the supply chain for health commodities, a 'ticking' sheet has been included in all ACT/RDT kits to track consumption. Since October 2012, when the booklets were included, the number of districts reporting has increased from 17% to 28%.

By late 2010, the roll-out of the electronic LMIS system, SIMAM, was complete and each of the ten provincial-level warehouses (and the three central warehouses in Maputo) had begun using the new LMIS. Unfortunately, the computer-based system has not yet been rolled out to any of the districts (as was originally planned).

It is important to note that both PMI and other donors have concentrated their support on strengthening the supply chain system at the central and provincial levels. To ensure that health facilities report consumption data routinely and experience fewer reduced stockouts and to achieve greater transparency throughout the system, it is important for the supply chain to reach district and facility levels.

Plans and justification

PMI will continue to work in collaboration with other USG partners and with the Global Fund to support improvements in key areas such as warehousing, supervision, and logistics management information systems. The latter will help increase data availability, collection, and quality. PMI will also provide technical assistance to CMAM to improve capacity to better liaise and strengthen communication and information exchange with the NMCP, continue to build-up human resources within CMAM, and improve warehousing management and logistics capabilities. Currently, CMAM does not enjoy the level of independent governance necessary to operate autonomously. However, PMI and USG supply chain partners will assist CMAM to better deal with the cross-cutting elements of a functional central medical store, which include management, finances, human resources, and operations.

With support from the Global Fund Round 8 Phase 2 health systems strengthening grant, CMAM will receive technical assistance to increase capacity for generating, tracking, and monitoring of warehousing documentation to better reconcile issues with consumption data in an attempt to mitigate the potential for leakage of commodities and to facilitate improved data collection for the LMIS. Additionally, CMAM's ability to conduct monthly periodic stock reconciliation and other routine quality assurance/control activities for basic warehouse management practices will be strengthened via technical assistance.

These activities align with MISAU's recently developed Logistics Plan of Action, a comprehensive operational plan for procurement and supply chain management. The USG, World Bank, and other partners have all committed to support the Logistics Plan of Action, and the Global Fund Round 8 health systems strengthening grant specifically addresses its implementation. Part of this plan will involve the tracking of information on ACT consumption and RDT use as monitored in the ACT/RDT kit system.

PMI will continue to support CMAM and strengthen its ability to implement the SIMAM LMIS, as well as fulfill MISAU's obligation under the Global Fund Round 8 grant for improved data collection on malaria commodities, by continuing with the ACT/RDT kitting system. Additionally, the End-use Verification Tool (*see Monitoring & Evaluation section*), together with the placement of the regional and provincial-level technical advisors will help information collection, aggregation, and timely delivery to CMAM to better inform all warehousing and procurement activities.

Proposed Activities with FY 2014 funding: (activity and costs covered in other sections).

BEHAVIOR CHANGE COMMUNICATION

NMCP/PMI Objectives

The objective of the NMCP's BCC activities is to ensure that by 2016 100% of the population is covered by key messages related to malaria prevention, diagnosis, and treatment. PMI supports a range of BCC activities aimed at promoting correct and consistent use of LLINs, increasing acceptance of IRS, and increasing adherence to treatment and prevention therapies.

In alignment with the GoM, PMI aims to achieve the following objectives in the next five years:

1. Strengthen the capacity of MISAU/DEPROS to effectively develop, implement, and coordinate malaria BCC strategies and approaches.
2. Build the capacity of local organizations to train religious leaders in BCC and community mobilization to reduce malaria prevalence.
3. Develop in-country capacity, within the NMCP and PMI implementing partners, to effectively monitor and evaluate the quality of BCC activities and their impact on desired behavioral outcomes.

Progress since PMI was launched

Since 2007, PMI has supported malaria social mobilization through a consortium of religious groups called the Inter-Religious Campaign Against Malaria (PIRCOM). In 2010, PMI shifted its capacity building support for BCC from the NMCP to DEPROS of MISAU to develop the overall malaria communication strategy. PMI has supported BCC for MIP activities, ITNs, and IRS. Although there was progress in some areas, BCC related to malaria prevention and control continues to be a significant gap in Mozambique. There is limited technical capacity for BCC at the NMCP, and the coordination between the malaria program and DEPROS is weak. Recently,

PMI partnered with WHO to complete the malaria BCC strategy, which has been finalized and approved.

PMI is the main donor supporting malaria BCC activities in Mozambique. Global Fund provides limited support to community-based BCC activities in the context of large-scale universal coverage campaigns of LLINs.

Progress in the past 12 months

In the past 12 months, PMI and other partners supported the completion and approval of the strategic plan for malaria BCC, which provides a framework for the implementation of all malaria BCC activities in Mozambique. PMI support for BCC activities has largely been through PIRCOM, which is working in Zambézia, Nampula, Sofala, Inhambane, and Gaza Provinces. During the past year, PIRCOM trained approximately 556 religious leaders and 1,102 volunteers on key malaria messages, who in turn have reached approximately 125,000 people. In addition, PIRCOM has trained 76 supervisors to monitor the effectiveness of the sermons and door-to-door visits by volunteers. Other PMI-supported BCC achievements to date include regular support for the Malaria Communication Group, including advising on the universal net coverage campaign and World Malaria Day 2013 commemoration with MISAU and PMI partners.

PIRCOM's main challenge has been to develop a good M&E plan for their BCC activities. PIRCOM received substantial support through PMI to improve its M&E operations. Additionally, an organizational capacity assessment for PIRCOM was conducted by external partners at the end of last year. This resulted in development of an institutional strengthening plan which identified organizational strengths and challenges but more importantly set strategies and plans for PIRCOM to effectively carry out activities. Areas highlighted for capacity development included developing key messages for BCC and M&E of BCC interventions. Resource mobilization was another area highlighted in the institutional strengthening plan as an opportunity for capacity development. Potential actions included developing and applying a resource mobilization plan and raising non-restricted resources.

PMI also implemented community mobilization activities in Zambézia Province to increase acceptance of the PMI-supported IRS program. The community sensitization activities were based on messages approved by the NMCP and included the involvement of local leaders in all steps of the campaign and the training of these leaders to mobilize their communities. Where available, APEs are involved in malaria BCC activities within their communities; however, few communities are covered.

The focus of BCC activities thus far in Mozambique has been on increasing the number of people with access to interventions, rather than identifying the behavioral barriers to accessing these interventions. As the interventions are scaled up, identifying these barriers will become a high priority. For example, support for APEs is being scaled up to increase access to diagnosis and treatment for those who don't seek care at health facilities. As these activities progress, the team may implement studies to identify reasons why those who do not access health facilities or are not reached by APEs are not seeking care. Similarly, PMI is planning to support a study to identify behavioral barriers to care for pregnant women. Results of post–universal ITN distribution surveys being conducted should help guide the implementation of BCC activities in areas with low net coverage and use.

Plans and Justification

PMI will continue to provide technical assistance to the NMCP and DEPROS to support MISAU efforts in BCC and will support community-based nongovernmental organizations to disseminate malaria prevention and treatment messages. PMI will work in close collaboration with other USG programs (PEPFAR, MCH) to strengthen the BCC capacity of DEPROS and will foster better collaboration and coordination between DEPROS and the NMCP. To support the NMCP, PMI is also working with other partners to ensure that the Malaria Communications Technical Working Group is meeting regularly. Special focus will be given to the dissemination of the recently approved strategic plan for malaria BCC. PMI will continue to support PIRCOM, which is covering half of Mozambique's eleven provinces, including Nampula and Zambézia Provinces, which are the two most populous provinces. PMI will also use the previous year's funds to carry out an independent assessment of PIRCOM's work and impact. Based on assessment findings, the team will revisit PIRCOM's strategies. PIRCOM will continue to be trained and mentored through the *Por Ti* project, based on the recommendations of the organizational capacity assessment and on the institutional strengthening plan.

To expand support beyond the provinces covered by PIRCOM, PMI will identify local or international nongovernmental organizations based at the provincial level to implement both facility-based and community-based BCC activities. In this expansion, PMI will prioritize those provinces and districts with existing partners funded through PEPFAR or other mechanisms, in order to leverage funds and increase the efficiency of the interventions. PMI will increase its support to Peace Corps so that it can be more engaged in the STOMP partnership. In line with STOMP best practices, Peace Corps Mozambique is making efforts to move its Peace Corps Volunteer Malaria Coordinator into Maputo to improve coordination among USG partners, MISAU, various implementing partners, and other Peace Corps volunteers.

Finally, PMI will continue to work in collaboration with USAID strategic information and health promotion colleagues to devise an M&E plan for the malaria BCC activities to help guide implementation and maximize impact of the BCC interventions. This will include an assessment of the effectiveness of BCC interventions using a combination of quantitative and qualitative measures.

Proposed Activities with FY 2014 funding: ($1,030,000)

1. Support community mobilization activities: PMI will continue to support religious leaders and volunteers to disseminate key malaria messages related to malaria prevention and treatment to communities in Zambézia, Nampula, Sofala, Inhambane. and Gaza Provinces through PIRCOM ($600,000);

2. Support provincial BCC activities: PMI will support four provincial-based organizations that will work through existing community networks and in close collaboration with the provincial health directorates to disseminate malaria-related messages in four additional provinces beyond the five provinces covered by PIRCOM ($300,000);

3. Support MISAU's malaria BCC activities: PMI will continue to support coordination of malaria BCC activities, dissemination of the malaria communication strategy, and strengthening DEPROS in the development, implementation, and coordination of BCC strategies and approaches. Support to MISAU will include provision of technical assistance to help identify critical behavioral barriers to the use and access of malaria interventions, develop key malaria messages, and update BCC guidelines ($100,000); and

4. Peace Corps collaboration: Continue to provide support to at least one Peace Corps volunteer to assist with LLIN logistics, to develop and disseminate radio spots with key malaria messages, and to work with PIRCOM provincial coordinators ($30,000).

MONITORING AND EVALUATION

NMCP/PMI Objectives

A sound M&E plan is a key component of the NMCP's goal of delivering data-driven malaria interventions throughout the country. Collecting and reporting quality data in a consistent and reliable manner is necessary to ensure that malaria interventions are applied in an efficient and effective manner and that they target the appropriate populations. Toward this goal, the NMCP finalized the 2012-2016 Monitoring and Evaluation Plan in 2012. Current sources of data that have and will continue to help guide programmatic decisions and evaluations of malaria programs in Mozambique are listed below.

Primary data sources for program evaluation and impact evaluation in Mozambique

	Year							
	2008	**2009**	**2010**	**2011**	**2012**	**2013**	**2014**	**2015**
HMIS	x	X	x	x	x	x	x	x
Sentinel sites	x	X	x					
Enhanced surveillance in IRS areas					x	x	x	x
DHS				x				
MICS	x							
INSIDA		X						
Joint INSIDA/MIS							x	
End-Use Verification Tool				x	x	x	x	x
LLIN universal coverage survey				x	x			
LLIN durability study		x	x	x	x			
Entomological monitoring in PMI IRS areas	x	x	x	x	x	x	x	x
Nationwide entomological sentinel sites						x	x	x

Historically, clinical and laboratory-confirmed malaria cases have been included in the reporting bulletin for notifiable diseases, *Boletim Epidemiologico Semanal, or Weekly Epidemilogic bulleting,* managed by the Department of Epidemiology. All public health facilities are expected to use this system to report the number of "confirmed" malaria cases on a weekly basis; however, even with the recent rollout of RDTs and updated case management guidelines, confirmed and clinical cases are not separately reported on a routine basis, limiting the quality of these data. Malaria morbidity data is also reported through the *Módulo Básico,* which is a routine health information system that flows directly to the *Departamento da Informacao da Saúde* (Department of Health Information), via the *Sistema de Informacao da Saúde* (Health Information System). Currently, *Modulo Basico* data are sent from health facilities to the district level where they are collated and transmitted to the provincial and national level. The system is intended to provide monthly data on malaria morbidity and mortality. It is also intended to capture indicators such as percentage of suspected cases receiving laboratory diagnosis and percentage of laboratory-confirmed cases receiving ACT treatment, which are important for program evaluation. To date, this system has proved to be of little use to NMCP programs.

In alignment with the above-stated goals of the NMCP, PMI aims to achieve the following objectives in the next five years:

1. Provide support for provincial and district level supervision and training of health workers and district and provincial M&E personnel on the collection and reporting of malaria indicators.
2. Support central level strengthening of the malaria M&E system to enable the implementation of scientifically data-driven malaria interventions by the NMCP.

Progress since PMI was launched

M&E System Strengthening: Multiple attempts have been made to strengthen the M&E system in Mozambique since PMI was launched in 2007. However, because the routine health information system, the *Modulo Basico,* collects indicators for tuberculosis, HIV, MCH, and malaria programs, efforts to improve or modify the system have proved to be complicated and time-consuming. The most recent update of the system, which occurred in 2012, is not expected to result in updated outpatient registers for several years. A consultant hired through support of the Southern African Development Community/Southern Africa Roll Back Malaria Network visited Mozambique in mid-2012 and created a comprehensive malaria database, which will be populated with new data elements collected from the existing outpatient registers as well as from other sources, specifically from new MCH registers, the pharmacy, and laboratory.

In early 2011, Malaria Control and Evaluation Partnerships in Africa (MACEPA) placed an M&E advisor in Mozambique to assist the NMCP and partners to better coordinate M&E activities, focusing mostly on the strategic and policy level activities (such as finalizing the draft M&E strategic plan as well as defining indicators). MACEPA has been working closely with PMI to ensure that efforts are not duplicated. The M&E advisor has played a central role in guiding the process of finalizing the M&E strategic document, as well as the National Malaria Policy and National Strategic Plan. The ongoing M&E coordination among stakeholders is critically important for the NMCP to have appropriate information to manage the program. The support from MACEPA ended in 2012, but PMI has made it a priority to ensure continuity of the M&E support provided through MACEPA, with plans to hire a two-year advisor to be placed at the NMCP with funds from the Office of the Global AIDS Coordinator .

Entomologic Monitoring: As outlined in the IRS section, PMI has provided a significant amount of support to build Mozambique's entomological capacity both at the central level and regionally. The PMI-supported central entomology laboratory and insectary at the INS in Maputo is operational and serves as the reference laboratory for in-country processing of mosquito material, such as polymerase chain reaction species identification of mosquito complexes, enzyme-linked immunosorbent assays for malaria-infected mosquitoes, monitoring for insecticide resistance and its mechanisms by both above-mentioned methods, and insecticide efficacy monitoring for IRS and LLINs nationwide. The PMI-supported entomology laboratory and insectary in Quelimane, Zambézia Province, serves as a regional center for entomologic monitoring and surveillance for IRS and LLIN activities in the central provinces of Mozambique. In a collaborative effort between PMI and the DPS in Zambézia, the Quelimane entomology laboratory has been staffed by four DPS personnel trained in basic entomologic field techniques, as well as insectary maintenance. PMI has provided funding for short-term technical assistance visits by entomologists from other African countries.

Similarly, the PMI-supported entomology laboratory in Pemba, Cabo Delgado Province, serves as a regional center for entomological monitoring and surveillance in the northern provinces. It is currently staffed by a DPS biologist who was trained in a WHO/PMI supported workshop in 2008, and by three technicians from the DPS. Due to the lack of entomologists at the central level, PMI in 2009 also hired an entomologist to provide two years of technical assistance to the NMCP on national entomology surveys and IRS surveillance in Zambézia.

End Use Verification Surveys: PMI-supported End-Use Verification assessments have been taking place since late 2011. This tool is used to assess the malaria-related commodities supply chain and availability of malaria-related commodities at the health facility level. Province and site selection is done in collaboration with the NMCP; approximately three provinces, including the provincial warehouse and two randomly selected district-level warehouses, are covered each quarter. Within each district, one urban health unit (health center or hospital), one rural health center, and one APE are also included. These assessments are seen as a way of identifying bottlenecks in the supply chain and addressing them in a timely manner, not a tool to assess national distribution performance. In addition, at the request of the NMCP, these surveys have been broadened to include a range of malaria activities. This includes laboratory, pharmacy, and case management components, where a sample of medical records from previous months are pulled and data are extracted to calculate various indicators on case management.

Initial data from the assessments done in 2011 and early 2012 showed that overall, stocks of AL from at least one of the four presentations were always found at the health facility level during the assessment, but stock-outs of all products, including AL, in the three months prior to the assessment were common at the health facility level (especially for RDTs and LLINs). Examples of some of the case management indicators observed were these: clinical diagnoses of malaria were still common (30% to 58%) and AL is being used for treatment of cases (94% to 100%).

Field Epidemiology & Laboratory Training Program (FELTP): The CDC-led FELTP activities in Mozambique are continuing with success. The two-year Master's level program in field and laboratory epidemiology started in August of 2010 with a cohort of five epidemiologists and six laboratorians, one of whom was mentored by the CDC PMI Resident Advisor and graduated in August of 2012. One of the newly accepted candidates for the second cohort is also being mentored by the CDC PMI Resident Advisor and will be assigned to the NMCP for her long-term project.

Progress in the past 12 months

M&E System Strengthening: Given the enormous pressure the NMCP is under to respond to donors on basic malaria indicators that should be collected through the routine health information system, the NMCP has implemented a national data collection system, which relies on abstracting malaria-specific data from existing registers and compiling this data into newly designed malaria data reporting forms. These forms are completed by health workers at the health facility level and sent to malaria "focal points" at the district level (*see Capacity Building Section*). The district focal point then compiles the data and sends it to the provincial level where data from all districts will be entered into a newly created malaria database. In mid-2012 MISAU led a roll-out of the new malaria data reporting system, which included national training of health workers to fill out the existing outpatient registers with new data elements, new data summary tools to compile health facility level data, and a new malaria database at the provincial level. These trainings, however, have largely taken place at the provincial level and have yet to result in a cascade of this information to the health facility level. As a consequence this system is still experiencing problems with consistency and quality of data collection and reporting, as well as sufficient staffing at the district and provincial levels to collect and enter the data and send it to the appropriate levels.

Entomologic Monitoring: PMI continued to support entomologic monitoring for MISAU's vector control activities in 2012, in addition to the entomologic monitoring done in Zambézia to inform PMI's spray program. For full entomologic monitoring results in Zambézia, including resistance testing, *see the IRS section*. Insecticide resistance testing was carried out in selected sentinel sites in seven provinces: Maputo, Inhambane, Manica, Sofala, Tete, Nampula, and Cabo Delgado. WHO resistance tests were conducted with bendiocarb, deltamethrin, DDT, and lambdacyhalothrin. Insecticide resistance varied between provinces. Lambdacyhalothrin resistance was noted in *An. gambiae* s.l. in Cabo Delgado (79% mortality) and in Tete (87.2% mortality). For *An. funestus s.l.*, bendiocarb resistance was found in Maputo (89%), and lambdacyhalothrin resistance was observed in Inhambane (88%). The INS and NMCP are collaborating in the molecular speciation of the mosquitoes collected for insecticide resistance testing.

In November 2012, the INS funded a three-week training course for an entomologist from their entomology team at the CDC. The training included molecular methods for mosquito species identification, molecular and biochemical methods for resistance mechanisms, and the bottle bioassay for evaluating insecticide resistance. As part of the molecular training, mosquitoes from the 2012 insecticide resistance testing were identified.

End Use Verification Surveys: The End-Use verification tool has been implemented four times in Mozambique (twice during the previous 12 months) and in theory, on a quarterly basis. Based on data collected from the End-Use Verification Tool thus far, a rebalancing of the ACT kits occurred (thereby contributing to better use of limited ACT supplies and ensuring less wastage). The decision was made to include RDTs in the kits. The project has hired an advisor for Zambézia Province and a regional advisor for the north to cover Nampula, Niassa and Cabo Delgado Provinces. With these peripheral-level advisors in place, the likelihood of data flowing from the rural level to the central level will increase. They will also be available to 'trouble shoot' apparent bottlenecks in distribution and to improve logistics-related coordination among relevant partners, both at the district level and centrally. Data from the most recent End-Use Verification Tool done in late 2012, which covered Nampula Province, Maputo Province, and the city of Maputo (n = 20 facilities/warehouses) demonstrated wide-scale stockouts of one or more of the four AL presentations (up to 67% of facilities were stocked out of multiple presentations). Of the facilities visited, 33% were stocked out of SP and 17% were stocked out of RDTs.

Field Epidemiology & Laboratory Training Program (FELTP): PMI is currently providing technical assistance to two FELTP-led studies. The first is an evaluation of MISAU's mass distribution campaigns for LLINs, which will take place in the fall of 2013. The study will mirror a similar one done in Sofala in 2009 (mentioned earlier) that validated both the effectiveness of the campaign in reaching its intended goals and the impact of the campaign on parasite prevalence of the targeted communities. The second study will attempt to identify barriers to IPTp uptake in selected provinces with the hope of finding specific barriers that can be targeted through BCC campaigns to increase IPTp uptake; this study is expected to take place in late 2013.

Plans and Justification

M&E System Strengthening: PMI will be providing long-term M&E technical assistance to the NMCP through the hiring of a full-time staff member who will be located within the NMCP and supervise the program's M&E activities through the Office of the Global AIDS Coordinator funding. With FY 2014 funding PMI will continue to provide provincial-level support for the M&E supervision begun with reprogrammed FY 2013 funds. This support will be focused initially in four targeted provinces (Cabo Delgado, Zambézia, Nampula, and one yet to be determined) with the aim of ensuring indicators that are vital to inform the NMCP's decisions on malaria interventions are being collected and reported with sufficient quality, consistency, and completeness.

Entomologic Monitoring: Because the new IMVCS also applies to national LLIN mass distribution campaigns and NMCP IRS activities, PMI will support the M&E of these activities through the expanded collection of key entomological data from nationwide sentinel sites, as well as by hiring staff at the central level to aid in the collection, processing, and evaluation of data collected through these activities.

End Use Verification Tool: With FY 2014 funds, PMI will continue to support implementation of the tool on a quarterly basis.

Field Epidemiology & Laboratory Training Program (FELTP): PMI will continue to support the FELTP program with FY 2014 funds.

Proposed Activities with FY 2014 funding: ($1,072,100)

1. Support for M&E supervision at the provincial level. Support for M&E supervision in four targeted provinces (Nampula, Zambézia, Cabo Delgado, and TBD), to ensure proper data collection and reporting practices from the facility to the central level ($300,000);

2. Entomologic monitoring for MISAU vector control activities. Support expanded entomologic monitoring nationwide in approximately 20 sentinel entomological sites (at least two in each province, one in an area of IRS and the other where LLINs are used) and processing of samples in reference lab ($250,000);

3. Support to reference laboratory technicians in INS, MISAU. Recruit and hire laboratory

technicians to conduct assays in entomological surveillance, diagnostic and immunology labs for entomological monitoring, and diagnostic quality assurance ($300,000);

4. Entomological technical assistance, including reagents and laboratory diagnostics materials ($35,000);

5. End-use verification. Support the implementation of the quarterly End-Use Verification surveys in a sample of health facilities and medical stores ($100,000);

6. FELTP. Support FELTP program with the participation of one or more NMCP staff ($75,000); and

7. M&E technical assistance. Support for M&E activities including those related to the 2014 MIS ($12,100).

CAPACITY BUILDING AND HEALTH SYSTEMS STRENGTHENING

NMCP/PMI Objectives

The NMCP is responsible for developing policy, establishing norms, and the planning, organization, and coordination of all malaria control activities in the country. Additional responsibilities include periodic assessment of the impact of malaria control, development of training materials on malaria case management for health workers at all levels, mobilization of domestic and external funds for malaria control activities, promotion of malaria awareness and advocacy, and leading operational research. However, the NMCP faces many challenges related to human resources at the central, provincial, and district levels. There are shortages of skilled health workers, a high turnover rate, and a lack of retention of health professionals at all levels.

Progress since PMI was launched

PMI is building capacity for malaria control at a number of levels. PMI Resident Advisors and implementing partners have provided technical and implementation support to the NMCP on a range of issues including development of the National Strategic Plan, the M&E Plan, the IMVCS and other key policy documents.

PMI supported an entomologist at the NMCP to coordinate all vector control activities outside of Zambézia Province (where PMI provides direct support for IRS activities). In Zambézia Province, PMI has been strengthening the capacity of the DPS to implement IRS activities and conduct entomologic monitoring through the establishment of a regional entomology laboratory and insectary, which is staffed by DPS personnel who work with PMI's partner on these activities. The regional entomology capacity to do entomologic monitoring/surveillance has also been supported by PMI through the establishment of an entomology lab in Pemba, Cabo Delgado. This lab is managed by the Provincial Malaria Chief from Cabo Delgado Province through support from the DPS, although more training and support for the maintenance of the laboratory is needed. The training is scheduled for FY 2013 through the entomology support provided by a CDC entomologist and will include insecticide resistance bioassays.

The National Reference Laboratory, the entomology laboratory, and an insectary at INS were refurbished and re-equipped with support from PMI. Three regional "training of trainers" for malaria microscopy were held in 2011 to establish a cadre of highly qualified master trainers. These trainings were led by CDC reference laboratorians and were very successful. Several technicians were chosen from among these master trainers to lead the national refresher training on malaria microscopic diagnosis. National training took place during 2011 and was finalized in November 2011; a total of 1,082 out of 1,200 laboratory technicians throughout Mozambique were trained. Moreover, PMI supported a needs assessment for the establishment of a quality control system for diagnostics in Mozambique; a draft guideline for such a system is awaiting approval. To complement this, two of the technicians working in the National Reference Laboratory traveled to Atlanta for a six-week training in molecular biology and other techniques that are seen as key activities of a diagnostic reference laboratory.

At the provincial level, the implementation and coordination of health services are the responsibility of the DPS, specifically the provincial medical chief. Each province has a provincial malaria chief, selected among a cadre of biologists trained by NMCP in 2008 and seconded to the provinces. In 2012 the NMCP identified focal points among existing personnel at the district level to be responsible for malaria activities, mainly in the area of reporting of malaria indicator data. This is an important step for improving the oversight of malaria-related activities as this identifies a person to be accountable for malaria-related activities.

Given the lack of professionally trained health workers, USG is contributing, along with other partners, to the "revitalization" of the APE system. The new APE system consists of community health workers who have been selected by their communities to undergo intensive four-month training on the prevention and treatment of common diseases, including malaria. Support for the APE revitalization comes from many partners, including UNICEF, USAID, World Bank, Irish Embassy, Malaria Consortium, Save the Children, and World Vision. The rollout of the APE trainings was divided into several rounds. Since the process began in 2011, 2,726 "revitalized" APEs have been trained.

Progress in the past 12 months

PMI supported the development of the Malaria Acceleration Plan and the Global Fund Round 9 Phase 2 proposal. This is a multiyear operational plan of the malaria control strategy, covering the period of 2014 to 2016, which gives guidance on the timing for implementation for specific activities, on the parties responsible for implementation, and on funding availability.

In addition to the FELTP program, PMI also supported in-service training and supervision of health workers at several levels in MIP, case management, laboratory diagnosis, and entomologic monitoring (see individual sections for more details).

During the past fiscal year, MISAU with support of USAID (using MCH funds), other donors, and other partners continued the expansion of the APE program, and 1,488 new APEs were trained nationwide. For the first time, data from the revitalized APE program (via UNICEF support with non-PMI funds) on malaria diagnosis and treatment at community level are available.

Plans and Justification

Strong and effective leadership by the NMCP will be critical to the success of Mozambique's malaria control efforts. As the number one killer of Mozambicans, malaria should be elevated within MISAU to a higher status. This will require strong leadership at the highest MISAU levels. To reach the NMCP targets, continued support along with close coordination with other partners and donors will be needed. This will be critical to strengthening the NMCP's capacity and that of other collaborating departments at the central, provincial, and district levels to plan, conduct, supervise, monitor, and evaluate malaria prevention and control activities.

To this end, PMI plans on decentralizing support to the provincial and district level. The objective of this approach is to improve implementation of malaria-related activities through the facilitation of supervision, distribution of commodities, and M&E. Exclusively supporting the central level limits PMI's ability to ensure that the activities implemented at the lowest level are done with any level of quality. This decentralization will be done through partners, especially local partners where they exist, and if possible directly to the DPS. In provinces where the USG has existing partners, efforts will be made to use these existing mechanisms, thereby avoiding duplication of efforts. The following activities will fall under this effort to decentralize PMI support: LLIN distribution to ANCs, IRS, case management supervision, BCC implementation, and M&E supervision. In addition, PMI will continue to support the kitting for APE commodities, entomology, data management and M&E activities for the NMCP and the National Directorate of Public Health, laboratory capacity building, and the FELTP program.

PMI will also support the hiring of a senior technical officer who will be seconded to the NMCP, with a focus on M&E (*see Monitoring & Evaluation section*). It is expected that this person will provide overall technical support to the program and serve as liaison between the NMCP and the Global Fund Unit. This activity will be initiated in 2013 with funds from the Office of the Global AIDS Coordinator.

Proposed Activities **with FY 2014 funding: (activity and costs covered in other sections)**

STAFFING AND ADMINISTRATION

Two health professionals serve as Resident Advisors to oversee PMI in Mozambique, one representing CDC and one representing USAID. In addition, one FSN works as part of the PMI team, and the Mission is in the process of hiring an additional FSN to support the program, as approved in the FY 2013 MOP. All PMI staff members are part of a single interagency team led by the USAID Mission Director or his/her designee in country. The PMI team shares responsibility for development and implementation of PMI strategies and work plans, coordination with national authorities, managing collaborating agencies and supervising day-today activities. Candidates for Resident Advisor positions (whether initial hires or replacements) will be evaluated and/or interviewed jointly by USAID and CDC, and both agencies will be involved in hiring decisions, with the final decision made by the individual agency.

The PMI professional staff work together to oversee all technical and administrative aspects of PMI, including finalizing details of the project design, implementing malaria prevention and treatment activities, monitoring and evaluation of outcomes and impact, reporting of results, and providing guidance to PMI partners.

The PMI lead in country is the USAID Mission Director. The two PMI resident advisors, one from USAID and one from CDC, report to the Senior USAID Health Officer for day-to-day leadership, and work together as a part of a single interagency team. The technical expertise housed in Atlanta and Washington guides PMI programmatic efforts and thus overall technical guidance for both RAs falls to the PMI staff in Atlanta and Washington. Since CDC resident advisors are CDC employees, responsibility for completing official performance reviews lies with the CDC Country Director, who is expected to rely upon input from PMI staff across the two agencies that work closely day in and day out with the CDC RA and thus best positioned to comment on the RA's performance.

The two PMI resident advisors are based within the USAID health office and are expected to spend approximately half their time sitting with and providing technical assistance to the national malaria control programs and partners.

Locally-hired staff to support PMI activities either in Ministries or in USAID will be approved by the USAID Mission Director. Because of the need to adhere to specific country policies and USAID accounting regulations, any transfer of PMI funds directly to Ministries or host governments will need to be approved by the USAID Mission Director and Controller, in addition to the PMI Coordinator.

Proposed Activities with FY 2014 funding: *($1,000,000)*

1. Management of PMI: Support to four staff members, including two senior Resident Advisors (one USAID and one CDC) based at the USAID Mission in Maputo, one senior Foreign Service National (project management specialist), and one mid-level Foreign Service National (project management assistant). The support includes all work-related expenses (e.g., salaries, travel, supplies, etc.), and mission-based expenditures, including USAID mission expenses incurred in the direct implementation of PMI activities ($1,000,000).

ANNEXES

Table 1

President's Malaria Initiative — Mozambique

Year 8 (FY 2014) Budget Breakdown by Partner ($)

Partner Organization	Geographic Area	Activity	Budget ($)
DELIVER	Nationwide	Procurement of 1.9 million LLINs for ANCs and EPI; Support for ANC and EPI net distribution from the port of entry to provinces to districts nationwide; Procurement of 10 million tablets of SP; Procurement of 11.3 million RDTs and additional microscopy kits, reagents, and microscopes if needed; Procurement of 4.4 million AL treatments; Strengthening of CMAM's capacity to forecast and manage antimalarial drugs and support distribution of ACTs through the kit system; Support warehousing and management logistics at regional/provincial/district levels; and Support the implementation of the End-Use Verification Tool	20,630,800
FORSSAS	Nationwide	Provide support to *Centro de Abastecimento* to strengthen the distribution system of LLINs through supervision and auditing; Central level support of APE program.	450,000
TBD	Nationwide	IRS campaign in six districts of Zambézia including procurement of PPE, spare parts, and IRS supplies; Support to NMCP IRS activities; Support for entomologic monitoring in PMI-supported districts in Zambézia; and Support for entomologic monitoring for MISAU vector control activities	3,850,000
MCHIP Associate Award	Nationwide	Support technical assistance and in service training and supervision of ANC staff in MIP	200,000
SCIP Nampula	Nampula Province	Support for provincial level supervision of ANC staff in MIP, malaria case management, BCC activities, and M&E.	300,000

SCIP Zambézia	Zambézia Province	Support for provincial level supervision of ANC staff in MIP, malaria case management, BCC activities, and M&E.	300,000
MalariaCare	Nationwide	Support supervision of laboratory diagnosis of malaria; Support supervision of clinical staff in malaria case management	500,000
CDC	Nationwide	Provide technical assistance for laboratory strengthening; Support for entomologic technical assistance; Support FELTP program; and Support for M&E activities, including MIS	139,200
PIRCOM	Five Provinces	Support PIRCOM to disseminate key malaria messages in five provinces	600,000
Peace Corps	Nationwide	Continue to provide support to at least one Peace Corps volunteer to assist with net logistics, to develop and disseminate radio spots with key malaria messages and to work with PIRCOM provincial coordinators	30,000
INS	Nationwide	Recruit and hire laboratory technicians to conduct assays in ento, diagnostic and immunology labs for ento monitoring, and diagnostic quality assurance	300,000
TBD	Two Provinces	Support for provincial level supervision of ANC staff in MIP, malaria case management, BCC activities, and M&E	600,000
TBD	Nationwide	Support coordination of malaria BCC activities, disseminate the malaria communication strategy and strengthen the DEPROS in the development, implementation and coordination of BCC strategies and approaches	100,000
Admin		Support in-country administrative expenses for CDC & USAID.	1,000,000
Total			**$29,000,000**

Table 2
President's Malaria Initiative
Planned Obligations for FY14 ($) 29,000,000

Proposed Activity	Mechanism	Budget	Commodities	Geographical area	Description
Procure LLINs	Deliver	6,680,800	6,680,800	Nationwide	Procurement of 1.9 million LLINs @ $3.5 per net targeting pregnant women and children under 5 distributing through ANCs and EPI
Support ANC & EPI LLIN distribution to districts	Deliver	1,500,000		Nationwide	Support for ANC & EPI LLIN distribution to all districts
Support to *Centro de Abastecimentos*	FORSSAS	200,000		Nationwide	Provide support to *Centro de Abastecimentos* to strengthen the distribution system of LLINs through supervision and auditing
SUBTOTAL ITNs		**8,380,800**	**6,680,800**		
Support IRS in six districts of Zambézia province	TBD	2,700,000		Zambézia	IRS targeted campaign in six districts of Zambézia covering 270,000 houses
Procure IRS commodities	TBD	250,000	250,000	Zambézia	Procurement of personal protective equipment, spare parts and other IRS supplies (excluding insecticides)
Support to NMCP IRS activities	TBD	500,000		Nationwide	Support training through a cascade approach and supervision of MISAU IRS activities
Support for entomologic monitoring in PMI IRS districts	TBD	150,000		Zambézia	Support ongoing entomologic monitoring in six IRS districts
SUBTOTAL IRS		**3,600,000**	**250,000**		

Activity	Implementer			Location	Description
Support technical assistance and in service training and supervision of ANC staff in MIP	MCHIP	200,000		Central level and targeted provinces	Integrated supervision of ANC health workers in prevention of MIP
Support in service training and supervision of ANC staff in MIP	SCIP NAMPULA SCIP ZAMBÉZIA TBD	300,000		Nampula, Zambézia, Cabo Delgado and TBD	Integrated in service training and supervision of ANC health workers in prevention of MIP
Procurement of SP	Deliver	400,000	400,000	Nationwide	Procurement of approximately 10 million tablets of SP
SUBTOTAL MIP		**900,000**	**400,000**		
Procure diagnostic supplies	Deliver	7,000,000	7,000,000	Nationwide	Purchase approximately 11.3 million RDTs
Support for malaria microscopy quality control	Deliver	50,000	50,000	INS	Provide laboratory supplies for malaria microscopy quality control
Support supervision of laboratory diagnosis of malaria	MalariaCare	250,000		Nationwide	Provide supervision of laboratory staff in malaria laboratory diagnosis, use of RDTs and including quality assurance
Provide technical assistance for laboratory strengthening	CDC	17,100		Nationwide	TDY for support of laboratory strengthening activities to NMCP, & quality control system support.
SUBTOTAL Diagnosis		**7,317,100**	**7,050,000**		
Procure artemether-lumefantrine	Deliver	4,000,000	4,000,000	Nationwide	Procurement and shipment of about 4.4 million AL treatments, including distribution to provinces

Activity	Partner	Budget	Geographic Area	Description
Strengthen MISAU antimalarial drug management system	Deliver	600,000	Nationwide	Strengthen CMAM's capacity to forecast and manage antimalarial drugs and support distribution of ACTs through the kit system
Support warehousing and drug management at regional/ provincial/district level	Deliver	300,000	Nationwide	Support warehousing and management logistics at regional/provincial/district levels
Support supervision of clinical staff	MalariaCare	250,000	Nationwide	Central level support supervision in malaria case management
Provincial case management (in health facilities and community level)	SCIP NAMPULA SCIP ZAMBÉZIA TBD	300,000	Nampula, Zambézia, Cabo Delgado and TBD	Provincial level supervisory activities for malaria case management in four targeted provinces
APE central level support	FORSSAS	250,000	Nationwide	Technical assistance to improve the efficiency of the APE program's coordination, increase the overall quality of the program, and improve the existing M&E systems.
SUBTOTAL Case management		**5,700,000**	**4,000,000**	
Support community mobilization activities through interfaith religious groups	PIRCOM	600,000	Zambézia, Nampula, Sofala, Inhambane and Gaza provinces	Support PIRCOM to disseminate key malaria messages in five provinces
BCC provincial support	SCIP NAMPULA SCIP ZAMBÉZIA TBD	300,000	Nampula, Zambézia, Cabo Delgado and TBD	Provincial level BCC activities for malaria messaging in four targeted provinces

Activity	Partner	Budget	Coverage	Description
Support MISAU's malaria BCC activities	TBD	100,000	Nationwide	Support coordination of malaria BCC activities, disseminate the malaria communication strategy and strengthen the DEPROS in the development, implementation and coordination of BCC strategies and approaches
Collaboration with Peace Corps	Peace Corps	30,000	Nationwide	Continue to provide support to at least one Peace Corps volunteer to assist with net logistics, to develop and disseminate radio spots with key malaria messages and to work with PIRCOM provincial coordinators
SUBTOTAL BCC		**1,030,000**		
Provincial support for M&E supervision	SCIP NAMPULA SCIP ZAMBÉZIA TBD	300,000	Four provinces	Support for M&E supervision from provincial in four targeted provinces (Nampula, Zambézia, Cabo Delgado and TBD)
Support for entomologic monitoring for MISAU vector control activities	TBD	250,000	Nationwide	Support expanded entomologic monitoring nationwide in sentinel entomological sites and process samples in reference lab
Support to reference laboratory technicians in INS, MISAU	INS	300,000	INS	Recruit and hire laboratory technicians to conduct assays in ento, diagnostic and immunology labs for ento monitoring, and diagnostic quality assurance
Support for entomologic technical assistance	CDC	35,000	Nationwide	Support for entomologic monitoring and training activities to include specific reagents and laboratory diagnostic materials

End-use verification	Deliver	100,000	Nationwide	Support the implementation of the End-Use Verification Tool in a sample of health facilities and medical stores
Field Epidemiology & Laboratory Training Program (FELTP)	CDC	75,000	Nationwide	Support FELTP program with the participation of one or more NMCP staff
M&E TA	CDC	12,100	Nationwide	Support for M&E activities, including MIS
SUBTOTAL M&E		**1,072,100**		
Support in-country administrative expenses	CDC & USAID	1,000,000	Nationwide	Staffing and general administrative support for PMI
TOTAL		**29,000,000**	18,380,800